Branson and Beyond is a travel guide for those of you who love country music and for those who just want a comfortable vacation filled with good entertainment.

You'll find special DON'T MISS!! listings, like a recommendation from a friend who's been there before.

You'll find BUDGET ALERT!! and HOW TO STRETCH $100!! which will help to keep a fun vacation from turning into a financial burden.

And there are TIPS! on ways to make life easy as you tackle unfamiliar territory.

For each locale there are maps to help you prevent needless wrong turns. There's all the information you'll need on how to get there, where to sleep and eat, and how to spend your time.

And for background that can make your trip more enjoyable, a section at the end of each entry presents a brief history of the area.

Those of you who love to plan ahead and savor future trips from the armchair will find plenty of phone numbers and addresses for making reservations or checking out the latest happenings.

And if you're a spontaneous traveler, keep this handy in case the billboards don't tell you all you want to know.

BRANSON *and* BEYOND

A COUNTRY MUSIC LOVER'S GUIDE TO VISITING BRANSON, MO NASHVILLE, TN PIGEON FORGE, TN

Kathryn Buckstaff

ST. MARTIN'S PAPERBACKS

A NOTE TO THE READER: While every effort has been made to ensure that this guide is accurate and up-to-date, inaccuracies and mistakes may nonetheless remain. You are urged to check on dates and prices beforehand to avoid inconvenience and surprises. Have fun!

BRANSON AND BEYOND

Copyright © 1993 by Kathryn Buckstaff.

Cover photograph of Dollywood by William Schemmel/Stock South; photograph of Mel Tillis by the author; photograph of The Grand Ole Opry by Michael Philip Manheim/Stock South.

ISBN: 0-312-95092-6

Printed in the United States of America

St. Martin's Paperbacks edition/April 1993

10 9 8 7 6 5 4 3 2 1

DEDICATION

This book is dedicated to the memory of
"The King of Country Music"
Roy Claxton Acuff
September 15, 1903 – November 23, 1992

Roy Acuff grew up in the hills of eastern Tennessee, the son of a country preacher. He longed to be a professional baseball player, but a series of sunstrokes left him bedridden for two years. Acuff didn't sing professionally until he was nearly thirty, when he started with the Tennessee Crackerjacks, who soon became the Smoky Mountain Boys.

Acuff said of his style, "I reared back and sang it. I did it like I was going for the cows in Union County." It was that heart, that lonely sound, that conviction, people first heard in 1938 from the stage of the Grand Ole Opry. Acuff sang on the Opry for fifty-four years, until his death of congestive heart failure at the age of eighty-nine. Along with songwriter Fred Rose, Acuff formed a music publishing company that put Nashville on country music's map.

Among the many honors Acuff received are his induction into the Country Music Hall of Fame and the Lifetime Achievement Award from the National Academy of Recording Arts & Sciences.

The sounds of Acuff's "Wabash Cannonball" and "Great Speckled Bird," among many other songs, will forever be mentioned when people talk about the roots of American country music.

ACKNOWLEDGMENTS

To all of those who provided me with information, and encouragement, my sincerest thanks. Of particular help:

* Bruce Cook
* Mel Tillis, who graces this book cover
* Boxcar Willie
* John Bowers and Dawn Erickson, Branson/ Lakes Area Chamber of Commerce
* Beth Wanser, Ozark Marketing Council
* Lisa Rau and Noel Hailey Perkin, Silver Dollar City
* Kay Powell, Department of Tourism, Pigeon Forge
* Paris Henry, Bohan Agency
* Cynthia Sanders, Nashville Chamber of Commerce
* Craig Lamb, Opryland USA
* Ellen Long, Dollywood

TABLE OF CONTENTS

CONTENTS

CONTENTS

CONTENTS

BRANSON and BEYOND

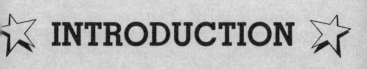

☆ INTRODUCTION ☆

★ *Branson and Beyond* is a travel guide for those of you who love country music and for those who just want a comfortable vacation filled with good entertainment.

You'll find special DON'T MISS!! listings, like a recommendation from a friend who's been there before.

You'll find BUDGET ALERT!! and HOW TO STRETCH $100!! which will help to keep a fun vacation from turning into a financial burden.

And there are TIPS! on ways to make life easy as you tackle unfamiliar territory.

For each locale there are maps to help you prevent needless wrong turns. There's all the information you'll need on how to get there, where to sleep and eat, and how to spend your time.

And for background that can make your trip more enjoyable, a section at the end of each entry presents a brief history of the area.

Those of you who love to plan ahead and savor future trips from the armchair will find plenty of phone numbers and addresses for making reservations or checking out the latest happenings.

And if you're a spontaneous traveler, keep this handy in case the billboards don't tell you all you want to know.

For everyone, there are surprises: how to get to Johnny Cash's home near Nashville, where to get your photograph taken with Mel Tillis or Boxcar Willie, how to get the best bargains in the outlet stores in Pigeon Forge.

And for those of you who know every word to "The Tennessee Waltz," there are tips on breaking into the business!

The guide covers Branson, Nashville, and Pigeon Forge. While there are other cities these days that have country music shows, Branson has emerged in the past two years as *the* place with the most live-performance theaters.

This little town in the Ozark mountains of southwest Missouri is where you'll find Roy Clark, Mel Tillis, Ray Stevens, Boxcar Willie, Andy Williams, Wayne Newton, and many other legends onstage in their own theaters. At the time of this writing, there were thirty theaters open in Branson, including the 4000-seat Grand Palace, where regulars Kenny Rogers, Glen Campbell, and Louise Mandrell welcome guests like the Oak Ridge Boys. Based on the phenomenally rapid growth of Branson, there are sure to be more theaters and more stars coming to the Ozark hills each year.

Of course, Nashville couldn't be omitted from a vacation guide for country music lovers. It's the home of the Grand Ole Opry, and still the recording center for country music. It's the city that produced stars from Hank Williams to Garth Brooks. It's the city where you can stand onstage at the Ryman Auditorium, where Roy Acuff sang for the first time in 1938.

Pigeon Forge is where shopping at more than 200 outlet stores will keep you busy between visits to the half-dozen country music theaters in town. And it's the home of Dollywood, the theme park co-owned by singer and actress Dolly Parton, who grew up in Sevier County, home of Pigeon Forge.

So dust off that sequined cowboy shirt you've never had just the right place to wear, put a Reba McEntire tape in the player, and get ready for a fabulous time in America's favorite country music centers.

☆ **BRANSON** ☆

★ When the folks at the *Wall Street Journal* dubbed Branson "the Broadway of Country Music," they weren't quite right. While there are 35 theaters on Broadway, there are only 31 theaters in Branson, if you don't include music theaters within theme parks. BUT there are more theater seats in Branson than on Broadway: 50,172 to Broadway's 42,458.

The theaters in this Ozark mountain hamlet provide entertainment from nine o'clock in the morning until eleven o'clock at night. The star-studded shows are the main attraction for the more than five million visitors from all over the country and around the world who pour into Branson each season. And while there are lots of big country stars performing here, diversity has become the newest trend, with pop singers Andy Williams, Wayne Newton, and Tony Orlando headlining at theaters.

On-stage entertainment isn't the only drawing card for Branson. Adjoining Branson are two large, beautiful lakes that brought visitors who enjoyed fishing and other lake sports for decades before the other attractions were established. The beauty of the Ozark mountains is still a big reason people come to Branson year after year.

It's also one of the friendliest tourist towns you'll ever visit. Here, nearly all the 3000 permanent residents benefit in some way from tourism, so they're more than delighted to see visitors arrive. And the friendly spirit catches on among attraction employees. Even drivers caught in rush-hour traffic on Country Music Boulevard will let someone into the line in front of them with a friendly wave. That's the way it's done in these hills.

Branson's a good vacation value too. A family of four can come for a few days of top-name entertainment and still have enough money left to get home. While there are several upscale lodges where rooms go for more than $100 a night, and restaurants where a couple can spend that much on an evening's meal and drinks, many motels are in the $35-to-$60-a-night range for two people.

There's plenty of good menu and buffet dining in the $5 to $10 range. And the shows range from $10 to $22 a ticket. That's great value for two hours of top-name talent. Especially compared to Broadway theater, which starts at $60 a ticket, and Las Vegas shows, which are $40 and up.

Other than packing in all the music shows you can, DON'T MISS!! *Silver Dollar City*. The 1880s theme park offers several in-park music shows daily, high-quality handcrafted gifts, and more of that friendly Ozarks charm.

Another DON'T MISS is Branson's old downtown. The shops and restaurants reflect the days when Branson was a lakeside resort, and it's a downtown that has remained a vital part of the town's appeal. The Taneycomo lakefront is a pleasant place to stroll and feed the ducks and Canadian geese that have made this their year-round home. Or ride up the river-shaped lake on the Lake Queen paddle wheeler.

Along the five miles of Country Music Boulevard, visitors of all ages will find delights from the arts and crafts in the Engler Block to plenty of miniature golf, go-carts, and White Water waterpark. Just north of the strip there are bargains galore in more than fifty outlet stores in Factory Merchants Mall.

For shoppers who'd rather poke around merchandise of the past, there are plenty of antique shops and flea markets. DON'T MISS!! downtown Hollister. Three miles south of Branson on U.S. 65, it's built to look like an old English village. The town of 2600 has lots of interesting curio shops.

GETTING THERE

Branson lies just a few miles north of the Missouri-Arkansas border in the western half of the state. The closest commercial airline flights land in Springfield, 45 miles north of Branson. Springfield Regional Airport is served by American Eagle, Northwest Airlink, USAir Express, Trans World Airlines, and United Airlines. Boone County Airport in Harrison, Arkansas, 40 miles south of Branson, is served by Lone Star Airlines, with flights from St. Louis and Dallas.

Rental cars are available at both airports. Boone County Airport is served by Avis; Springfield's airport by Avis, Budget, Hertz, and National. Reservations for the cars are a good idea during summer and fall months.

U.S. 65 from Harrison or Springfield leads to Missouri 76, the main path through the entertainment district.

GETTING AROUND

Traffic on the five-mile strip often moves slowly, partly because everyone wants to look at all the shops, theaters, and attractions along the way. So it's a good idea to allow plenty of time to reach your destination.

The road is three lanes—one eastbound, one westbound, with the center designated as a turning lane. It's against city ordinance to travel in the center lane.

Courtesy helps. Drivers on the Branson strip are noted for allowing cars into the lanes of traffic.

Several new streets and alternate routes give drivers the option of bypassing portions of the strip. It means going an extra mile or two, but it can save time, and give you a look at off-the-beaten-track businesses too.

TIP! I recommend taking a few minutes to study the maps in this section to determine the easiest way to get where you're going.

Heaviest traffic times on the strip are in the early afternoon (noon to 1:30); from 6:30 to 8 P.M., when visitors are on their way to restaurants and theaters; and from 10 to 11 P.M., after the theaters close for the evening.

With a little planning—and a close look at a map of the area—visitors can avoid the traffic jams just like the natives do.

Other options: If you want to leave the car at the motel, the *Branson Trolley Company* operates a daily schedule with stops all along the strip. The trolleys run from 6 A.M. until everyone's delivered home after the shows let out. An all-day pass costs $5 for adults, $2.50 for children 12 and under; a one-way ride is $1.50 for adults, 75 cents for children. For information, call 417-334-8759.

Branson City Cab service: In addition to delivering passengers, they will pick up food orders from restaurants for delivery to motels. Phone: 417-334-5678.

Roadsters U-Drive: For a little Gatsby-style fun, you can rent a Model A roadster replica. It seats four adults, including the rumble seat. They even provide a map of scenic back roads. Opens March 15. The $24.95 an hour includes gasoline and unlimited mileage. Rates for additional hours decrease. Located at Long's Wax Museum, 3030 Highway 76 West. Phone: 417-335-2337, 800-457-4665.

Weather: While summer days can reach into the nineties or even edge over 100 degrees during a hot spell, evenings in the Ozark mountains bring welcome relief and often a breeze. Even for a summer visit, a sweater or light jacket might be nice for sitting on the porch and watching the fireflies rise out of the grass.

January and February are the months when winter weather may rear its ugly head. While most winters are mild, with daytime temperatures in the fifties and nights around freezing, there is the possibility of snow or an occasional ice storm here. Snowfall usually means two to six inches, but can stay on the ground for a week or more.

Dress: While Branson is a casual-dress vacation destination, there are restaurants where dressing up can be fun, although none require a jacket and tie. If you like wearing sequined western shirts, or have jeans with fringes down the side that you've never gotten to wear around East Poughkeepsie, bring them to Branson. Here, it's not unusual to see ordinary folks dressed up like they're ready to go onstage at a country music show.

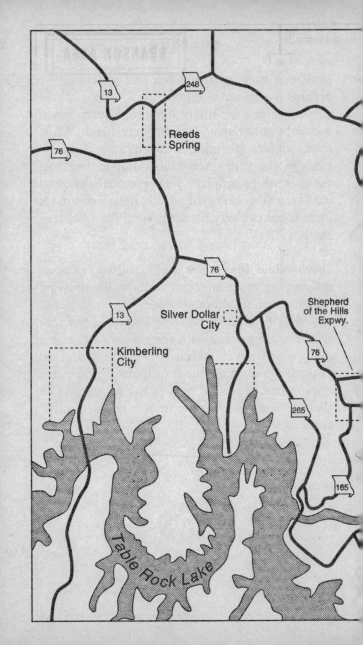

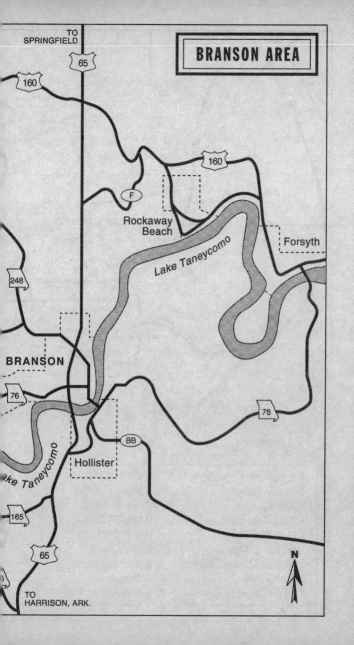

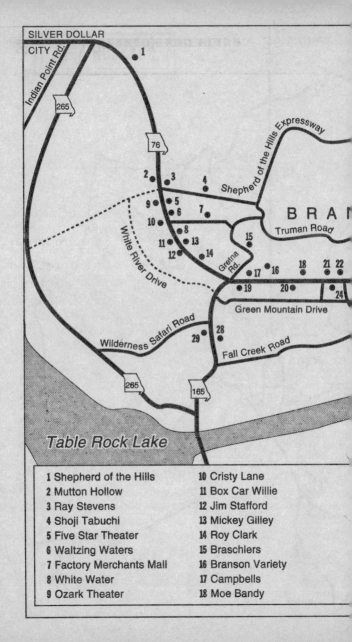

SILVER DOLLAR CITY

Indian Point Rd.

265

76

Shepherd of the Hills Expressway

Shepherd of the Hills

BRA N

Truman Road

White River Drive

Gretna Rd.

Green Mountain Drive

Wilderness Safari Road

Fall Creek Road

265

165

Table Rock Lake

1 Shepherd of the Hills
2 Mutton Hollow
3 Ray Stevens
4 Shoji Tabuchi
5 Five Star Theater
6 Waltzing Waters
7 Factory Merchants Mall
8 White Water
9 Ozark Theater

10 Cristy Lane
11 Box Car Willie
12 Jim Stafford
13 Mickey Gilley
14 Roy Clark
15 Braschlers
16 Branson Variety
17 Campbells
18 Moe Bandy

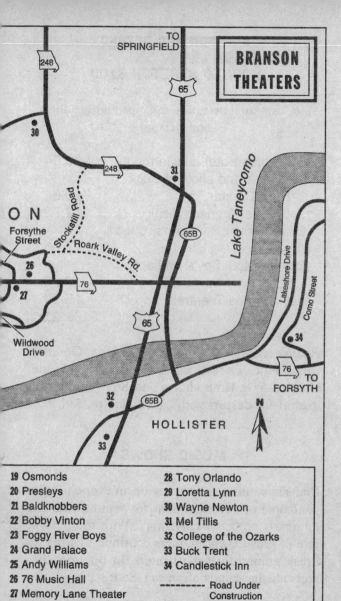

TO
SPRINGFIELD

248

65

BRANSON
THEATERS

30

248

31

65B

Lake Taneycomo

O N
Forsythe
Street

Stockstill Road

Roark Valley Rd.

26

27

76

65

Wildwood
Drive

Lakeshore Drive

Como Street

34

76
TO
FORSYTH

32

65B

N

HOLLISTER

33

19 Osmonds	28 Tony Orlando
20 Presleys	29 Loretta Lynn
21 Baldknobbers	30 Wayne Newton
22 Bobby Vinton	31 Mel Tillis
23 Foggy River Boys	32 College of the Ozarks
24 Grand Palace	33 Buck Trent
25 Andy Williams	34 Candlestick Inn
26 76 Music Hall	
27 Memory Lane Theater	---------- Road Under Construction

HOW TO STRETCH $100

(Costs include taxes and tips and are for
one person)

Ye English Hotel (single room)	$36.04
Breakfast and show at Buck Trent Theater	15.84
Souvenirs: Branson T-shirt	12.72
Lunch, Sugar Hill Farms, Cobb salad	7.06
Dinner, McGuffey's barbecued ribs	13.65
Ray Stevens Theatre	15.90
	$101.21

Possible splurge: Dinner at Dimitris Gourmet Restaurant. Caesar salad, prepared tableside; Grecian-style lamb chops; and Strawberries Romanoff for dessert with café amaretto: $34.50.

MUSIC SHOWS

Branson's music shows provide an ever-changing panorama of entertainment for visitors with the emphasis on "ever-changing." With the present rate of growth, entertainers continue to arrive to break ground for new theaters. In Branson, theaters change hands often too. So it's a good idea while you're making your Branson plans to check with the Chamber of Commerce for the latest information on who's playing where and when.

While Branson's first shows were strictly hard-core traditional country music, the recent growth has brought diversity. Andy Williams, the Osmond Brothers, and John Davidson have proven that fans want the variety that Branson offers.

Many of the performers here have their own trademark. Count on Ray Stevens and Jim Stafford to keep you laughing. Plan on Mickey Gilley's ballads to soften your heart. And check out Boxcar Willie for pure country with that lonesome railroad-blues feeling.

One of the pleasant surprises for first-time visitors to Branson is that you don't have to be a fan of country music to enjoy these shows. This is entertainment, folks. You may not be able to name a single Mel Tillis hit, but Tillis is a consummate performer. He, like others, have gathered fine backup musicians. His 2100-seat theater, built in 1990, is comfortable. State-of-the-art sound, lighting and special effects—like the forty-foot-wide rain curtain (yes, it's real water!)—make the show a pleasure for all tastes.

DON'T MISS!! *any of the shows*. I haven't put any individual DON'T MISS!! flags in this section because every show is good. If you have favorite stars, see them. Or pick the show closest

21

to your motel. See as many as you can. You can take in three a day if you've got the stamina, and many visitors do exactly that.

Don't shy away from a show starring someone you've never heard of. Don't miss the original variety shows, like the Presley's and the Baldknobbers, that started the entertainment move in Branson. Competition has become fierce, so the theaters spend money to keep the quality high. If you have a problem with a show, don't hesitate to ask for a refund. Most are eager to keep customers satisfied.

Season length: In the past, the Branson season ran from May through October, but no more. Now many theaters open in mid-February, and all of them run through the close of Ozark Mountain Christmas in late December. Several also feature New Year's Eve shows and parties. The theaters operate shows six or seven days a week from mid-April through October. Some offer performances only on Thursday through Sunday during February, November, and December.

Within a year or two, as Branson continues to grow, expect most theaters to stay open year-round, or to close only for a couple of weeks in winter.

Reservations: All the theaters listed here offer reserved seating, which can be essential since many shows sell out, sometimes weeks in advance. Reservations can be made by phone, and all the theaters accept major credit cards. TIP! All the theaters are able to accommodate wheelchairs. Several are equipped for the hearing impaired.

Andy Williams Moon River Theatre: The crooner hasn't lost his touch. Accompanied by a full orchestra, Williams performs the concert-style show of all his old favorites along with new tunes. Occasional special guests join Williams onstage. His smooth style highlights his beautiful 2055-seat theater. Built in 1992, the theater has won landscaping awards and architectural recognition for its classy decor. Expect great acoustics. The theater opens April 9 with shows at 3 and 7 P.M., Tuesdays through Sundays. Admission: $17; children under 12, $8. Address: 2500 Highway 76 West. Phone: 417-334-4500.

Baldknobbers Hillbilly Jamboree: Branson's first music show began in 1960 in a 50-seat auditorium in City Hall. In 1968 the Mabe family built an 865-seat theater on Missouri 76 to house their family show. It was the second theater built on Country Music Boulevard. Renovations over the years have expanded the theater to 1700 seats and have kept the sound and production values high. But the show retains the variety flavor of the early productions. Top-notch musicians and entertainers provide a lively show. Opening March 6. Warm-up shows begin at 7:15, regular performance at 8 P.M., Mondays through Saturdays. Admission: $13; children under 12, $5. Address: 2845 Highway 76 West. P.O. Box 972, Branson, MO 65616. Phone: 417-334-4528.

Bobby Vinton's Blue Velvet Theater: This 1300-seat theater is scheduled to open by June 1, 1993. Vinton, best known for his hits "Red Roses for a Blue Lady," "Mr. Lonely," and "Blue Velvet," will have a big band backing his smooth voice. He plans to perform shows Thursdays through Tuesdays at 2:30 and 7 P.M. Call the theater for exact schedules and prices. Address: 2701 Highway 76 West, across from the Grand Palace. Phone: 417-334-2500.

The Boxcar Willie Theatre: This man can whistle like a train without a whistle in his mouth. It's an amazing trick and fits with his railroading songs and "World's Favorite Hobo" image. The Air Force veteran opened his 900-seat theater in 1987. Boxcar loves to sing the traditional music of Hank Williams Sr., the original Jimmy Rodgers, Ernest Tubb, and leave the cross-overs to others. DON'T MISS!! Boxcar's Railroad and Airplane Museum next door to the theater. Open April 30 through October 30, with shows Mondays through Saturdays at 8 P.M.; matinees at 2 P.M. Tuesdays. Admission: $15; children under 12, $7. Address: 3453 Highway 76 West, Branson, MO 65616. Phone: 417-334-8696; 417-334-8656; 800-942-4626.

Branson's Variety Theater: This 730-seat theater located behind the Riverboat Motel has three shows a day Tuesdays through Saturdays from January 7 through New Year's Eve.

10 A.M. "The Second Generation," a variety show featuring Warner Brothers recording star John Wesley Probst.

2 P.M. "Branson Now" features country singers the Howard Brothers, formerly with Merle Haggard.

8 P.M. "Showcase of the Stars" will feature various artists for limited engagements. Call the theater for the schedule.

Admission to each show is $12; children under 12 free. Address: 3105 Highway 76 West, Branson, MO 65616. Phone: 417-336-4709.

Braschler Quartet Music Show: Since 1984 this quartet has been warming hearts with gospel favorites and country tunes. Opening April 9 with shows daily at 8:15 P.M. through mid-December. Beginning in May, 2 P.M. gospel matinees on Tuesdays and Thursdays.

The Sons of the Pioneers, who have been singing country western classics for nearly sixty years, will perform either a morning or afternoon show. Call the theater for the schedule. Admission: $12; children under 12 free. Located a half mile north of Missouri 76 at 310 Gretna Road, Branson, MO 65616. Phone: 417-334-4363.

Buck Trent Breakfast Theatre: Buck Trent, twice named Instrumentalist of the Year by *Music City News*, was with the cast of the Porter Wagoner Show with Dolly Parton for twelve years. He also was a star of "Hee Haw" for nine years. In 1981 Trent fell in love with the Ozarks. Now he starts his banjo pickin' early in the day. There's buffet breakfast at 8 A.M., and his show begins at 9 A.M., leaving plenty of time for more activities later. He performs at Tommy's Restaurant and Lounge off U.S. 65, three miles south of Branson in Hollister. He opens March 5 for performances Fridays and Saturdays through mid-April. Mid-April through mid-December, he performs daily except Sundays. Admission, including breakfast: $14.95; children 12 through 5, $8.95; children under 4 free. HCR 2, Box 890, Hollister, MO 65672. Phone: 417-335-5428 or Tommy's at 417-334-4995.

Campbell's Ozark Country Jubilee: This 880-seat theater presents shows at 10 A.M., 2 P.M., and 8 P.M.

The 10 A.M. show features Bob Nichols' lively "Ozarks Morning Show." For details on other shows and prices, contact the theater. Opening April 16. Address: 3115 Highway 76 West, Branson, MO 65616. Phone: 417-334-6400; 800-365-5833.

Cristy Lane Theatre: Cristy Lane, best known for her smash hit, "One Day at a Time," is a soft crooner and does lots of favorites, including a tear-jerking rendition of "Danny Boy." The theater operates from March 2 through New Year's Eve. Lane appears Tuesdays through Saturdays at 7:30 P.M. Admission: $16.50; children under 12, $10.

At 10 A.M. Tuesdays through Saturdays, see Ferlin Husky, best known for his hit recording of "On the Wings of a Dove." Admission: $15; children under 12, $10.

A matinee called "Blondes, Blondes, Blondes" is performed Tuesdays through Saturdays at 1 P.M., and Sundays and Mondays at 7:30 P.M. The lively Las Vegas–type show features a salute to blonde singers from the twenties through the nineties. Admission: $15; children under 12, $10. Address: 3600 Highway 76 West. P.O. Box 630, Branson, MO 65616. Phone: 417-335-5111.

Five Star Theatre: Plans for this 2000-seat theater located toward the west end of the strip are incomplete. For current scheduling information, call the Branson/Lakes Area Chamber of Commerce at 417-334-4084; 900-884-2726.

Foggy River Boys Theatre: The Foggy River Boys quartet have been performing in Branson since 1974 and are a favorite of return visitors as well as area residents. The 893-seat theater opens April 1 for shows daily except Sundays, at 8 P.M. Admission: $11; children under 12, $3. Address: 2325 Highway 76 West. P.O. Box 66, Branson, MO 65616. Phone: 417-334-2563.

The Grand Palace: Built by Silver Dollar City, Inc., in 1992, the lavishly appointed Palace seats 4000. Louise Mandrell, Glen Campbell, Kenny Rogers, and the Oak Ridge Boys are regulars scheduled throughout the season. There also are limited engagements by visiting guest artists.

> March 12, 19, 26 at 8 P.M.
>
> March 13, 20, 27 at 2 and 8 P.M.
>
> April 2, 9, 16, 18, 23, 25 at 8 P.M.
>
> April 3, 10, 17, 24, 30 at 2 and 8 P.M.
>
> May through October, two shows daily at 2 and 8 P.M.
>
> November 5 through December 19 at 8 P.M., shows Fridays through Sundays; Saturdays at 3 P.M.
>
> Admission for regular shows: ages 12 and up is $23, $19, $15; ages 4 through 11 is $13, $11, $9.
>
> Limited engagements admissions: ages 4 and up is $26, $22, $18.

Address: 2700 Highway 76 West, Branson, MO
65616. Phone: 417-334-7263.

Jim Stafford Theatre: Stafford bought his 818-seat
theater in 1991. The craftsman of comedy, who
wrote for the Smothers Brothers and hosted
TV's "Those Amazing Animals," may be best
known for his hits "Spiders and Snakes" and
"Cow Patty." Audiences will laugh. There's no
way to avoid it when Stafford gets rolling. In
fact, he usually breaks up too, despite doing
daily shows at 8 P.M. from mid-April through
mid-December. The theater opens for 8 P.M.
shows Fridays through Sundays on February 19.
Beginning in May, Stafford does matinees at 2
P.M. on Mondays, Wednesdays, and Saturdays.

Crooner and television star John Davidson
also performs matinees. Call theater for exact
schedule. Admission: $15; children 6 through 12,
$7.50; under 6 free. Address: 3446 Highway 76
West, Branson, MO 65616. Phone: 417-335-8080;
800-677-8533.

Loretta Lynn's Butcher Holler: This theater featuring the ever-dynamic and classy Loretta Lynn is
scheduled to open on Missouri 165, one mile
south of Missouri 76, in the summer of 1993. For
more information, call the Branson/Lakes Area
Chamber of Commerce at 417-334-4084.

Mel Tillis Theatre: When this stuttering celebrity
—who never stutters when he sings—built his

2100-seat theater in 1991, he spared no expense for production equipment. The highlight is a forty-foot-wide "rain curtain." It's real water that falls across the front of the stage. Don't worry if you sit in the front row. The water is chilled to prevent evaporation and treated with glycerine so it never splashes. The theater opens for weekends on February 19 with shows at 2 and 8 P.M. Beginning April 1, through mid-December, Tillis performs Tuesdays through Saturdays at 2 and 8 P.M. Sundays and Mondays, Marie Osmond is the special guest, tentatively scheduled for appearances on Sundays and Mondays at 2 and 8 P.M. Call the theater for exact schedules. Admission: $15.50; children under 12, $5. The theater is located on U.S. 65 at Missouri 248, one mile north of Missouri 76. P.O. Box 1626, Branson, MO 65616. Phone: 417-335-8089.

Memory Lane Theatre: This 450-seat theater inside the Branson Mall between Wal-Mart and Consumers features three shows daily:

10 A.M. The morning show features the Blackwood Quartet doing favorite country tunes and lots of gospel songs. Also featured are the Blackwood Sisters Quartet. The girls range from age six to 12. The quartets perform Tuesday through Sunday mornings plus a 2 P.M. show on Sundays.

At 2 P.M. Mondays through Saturdays, see the Texans. This quartet has been entertaining

Branson audiences for more than a decade. Featured in their variety is comedian Boy Howdy.

At 7 P.M. catch "Back In Time," a variety show featuring tunes from the fifties and sixties as well as gospel favorites. Included in the show are ragtime piano player Pinky Hull, and Elvis Presley impersonator Dennis Waugh with his "Memories of Elvis." The program is presented Tuesdays through Saturdays. Admission for each show, $12; children under 12, $5. Address: 2206 Highway 76 West, Box E-202, Branson, MO 65616. Phone: 417-335-3777.

Mickey Gilley's Family Theatre: Opened in 1990, Gilley offers his distinctive brand of soulful ballads like hits "Roomful of Roses" and "Stand by Me" in this 900-seat theater. The theater opens April 2. Gilley will be performing at 8 P.M. Fridays and Saturdays, and at 3 P.M. Sundays through April 18. Conway Twitty will perform 3 and 8 P.M. shows April 23, 24, 25, and 30. Beginning in May, Gilley and Twitty will perform shows at 3 and 8 P.M. on alternate weeks through December 5. Call the theater to see who's playing. Admission: $16; children under 12, $9. Address: 3455 Highway 76 West, Branson, MO 65616. Phone: 417-334-3210; 800-334-1936.

Moe Bandy's Americana Theatre: "Bandy the Rodeo Clown" sings his hits and more, including his 1972 hit "I Just Started Hating Cheating

Songs Today," in this 900-seat theater. The theater's name comes from the song "Americana," which George Bush picked for his unofficial 1988 campaign theme song. Have a question ready to ask Moe during intermission when he chats with the audience. The theater opens April 1 with shows at 2 and 8 P.M. Thursdays through Saturdays. In May, shows daily at 2 and 8 P.M. except Sundays. Special guests often perform on Sundays. Admission: $15; children under 12 free. Address: 2905 Highway 76 West. P.O. Box 1987, Branson, MO 65616. Phone: 417-335-8176; 800-424-2334.

Osmonds Family Theatre: This talented group of brothers are loved from their childhood appearances for seven years on television's "The Andy Williams Show." They've still got the harmony, and those gleaming smiles. Lots of lively treats in this show, including occasional visits from the Osmonds—The Second Generation, a quartet of Alan Osmond's sons. Opening February 18 for shows at 3 and 8 P.M. Thursdays through Saturdays. Beginning in March, shows Mondays through Saturdays at 3 and 8 P.M. Admission: $15.50; children under 12, $5. Address: 3216 Highway 76 West. P.O. Box 7122, Branson, MO 65616. Phone: 417-336-6100.

Presley's Mountain Music Jubilee: The Presley family were the first to open a theater on Missouri

76. In 1967 the musical family opened a 363-seat theater that has expanded to seat 2000. Many fans return to Branson year after year and never miss Presley's sparkling program of traditional and new country music. Comedians Herkimer and Harley Worthit may seem to be a few bricks short of a full load, but they don't miss the punch lines, and they keep the audience laughing. Three generations still perform together nightly at 8 P.M., with a warm-up show beginning at 7:30 P.M. Admission: $13.50; children under 12, $6. Address: 2920 Highway 76 West, Branson, MO 65616. Phone: 417-334-4874.

Ray Stevens Theatre: Stevens and his band, the French Fried Far-Out Legion Band, opened his 2000-seat theater in 1991. The theater features a desert motif, reminiscent of his hit, "Ahab the Arab." For six years in a row Stevens has been named "Comedian of the Year" by the Nashville Network. He keeps things moving with favorites like "The Streak," "Mississippi Squirrel Revival," and "Everything Is Beautiful," in addition to spectacular lights and special effects. The theater opens May 1 for performances at 3 and 8 P.M. daily except Sundays. Admission: $15.95; children under 12, $9.95. Address: 3815 Highway 76 West, Branson, MO 65616. Phone: 417-334-2422.

Roy Clark's Celebrity Theatre: Branson gained its first widespread national attention in 1983 when Roy Clark, longtime host of "Hee Haw," opened his 1140-seat theater. Clark performed 100 dates a year and brought in other stars. For some, like Mel Tillis and Ray Stevens, it whetted their appetite for Branson. The theater opens April 2 for weekends with daily shows at 3 and 7 P.M. beginning in May. Roy features lots of guest stars too, so call to check the schedule. Admission: $16; children under 12, $5. Dinner show (same show from private table with prime rib dinner) $30.50. Stay after the show for dancing and cocktails in Roy's Loft.

At 10 A.M. the theater presents "Jennifer in the Morning," starring lively songstress Jennifer Wilson, daily except Sundays. Wilson sings and dances and is joined by impressionist Jeff Brandt and her band, the Prime Time Pickers. Admission: $11; children 13 and under, free. Address: 3431 Highway 76 West, Branson, MO 65616. Phone: 417-334-0076; 800-352-5275.

76 Music Hall: In 1990 the Hall became the first theater to offer three shows daily in this 553-seat theater. *Now it's up to four shows a day!* In January, through February 18, you can see the Brumley Music Show at 8 P.M. Mondays through Saturdays. Albert Brumley Jr. carries on in the tradition of his father, Albert Sr., who wrote the hit song "I'll Fly Away" in 1932. From February 19 through March 17 see the Brumleys at 1:30 P.M., and the Memory Makers at 8 P.M. Mondays through Saturdays. On Sundays it's the Texas Gold Miners at 8 P.M.

From April through December 18, the Mondays through Saturdays lineup is the Brumley Music Show at 10 A.M., the Down Home Country Show at 1:30 P.M., the Texas Gold Miners at 4 P.M., and the Memory Makers at 8 P.M. On Sundays, the Sunday Gospel Jubilee performs at 2 P.M., with the Texas Gold Miners at 8 P.M.

Admission to each show is $12; children under 12 free. Address: 1919 Highway 76 West, Branson, MO 65616. Phone: 417-335-2484.

Shoji Tabuchi Theatre: A unique entertainer, Tabuchi continues to have one of the best-loved shows in town. The classically-trained fiddle player moved to the United States twenty years ago to pursue his dreams of country music after hearing Roy Acuff perform at the university Tabuchi attended in Osaka, Japan. The show in his new 2000-seat theater is a broad mix of musical styles and lavish production numbers punctuated by Shoji's own style of comedy. If you attend the theater, DON'T MISS!! the women's rest room. Complete with an Italian marble fireplace and orchids in bud vases, it is a fancy privy. (Men are taken on tours after the shows.) The theater opens April 2 with shows Mondays through Saturdays at 3 and 8 P.M. Closed on Sundays. Admission: $22; children under 12, $14. Located on Shepherd of the Hills Expressway, just north of Missouri 76. HCR 1, Box 755, Branson, MO 65616. Phone: 417-334-7469.

Ozark Theater: Plans for this 1465-seat theater are incomplete except for Ozark Mountain Christmas when pianist Dino Kartsonakis will bring five grand pianos and lots of singers and dancers for his traditional "Pianorama." The keyboard wizard will perform November 4 through New Year's Eve, Thursdays through Sundays at 2 and 7 P.M. Admission: $16.50; children under 12, $9.50. Call the theater for current scheduling. Address: 3800 Highway 76 West, Branson, MO 65616. Phone: 417-334-0023.

Tony Orlando's Yellow Ribbon Theater: Due to open July 4, 1993, this 2000-seat theater on Missouri 165 one mile south of Missouri 76 is situated in a grove of oak trees; perfect for the singer whose 1973 hit, "Tie a Yellow Ribbon 'Round the Ole Oak Tree," has become the anthem for freedom and homecoming in America. Plans are for this enthusiastic showman to perform daily at 2 and 8 P.M. Tentative ticket prices are $15.92; children under 12, $6.41. For more information, write: Yellow Ribbon Theater, The Falls, Highway 165, Branson, MO 65616. Phone: 417-335-8669.

Waltzing Waters: Identical twin singers John and Paul Cody, who look like a stunning combination of Rhett Butler and Robert Goulet, do a variety of popular music with lighted, dancing water as a background. From May through October, the Codys perform with the 40,000 gallons of dancing waters daily except Sundays at 10 A.M. and 1 P.M. The water show, minus the Codys, runs every hour from 9 A.M. to 11 P.M. May through October. The dancing waters, again minus the Codys, is open the remainder of the time, from October to May, with shows on the hour from 10 A.M. to 8 P.M. Admission: Water show only, $4; children under 12, $2. For the Codys' performances, $7; children under 12, $3.50. On the west end of Highway 76 West. P.O. Box V, Branson, MO 65616. Phone: 417-334-4144.

Wayne Newton Theatre: This new 3000-seat theater, set to open May 1, is styled like a Victorian mansion in the tradition of houses Newton saw while growing up in Virginia. The show primarily focuses on Newton, who enjoys developing a close rapport with theatergoers. He's backed by a 25-piece orchestra. The theater will operate Mondays through Saturdays, with performances at 3 and 8 P.M. There is no matinee on Fridays, and the theater is closed Sundays. In November and December, Newton will do shows Thursdays through Saturdays. He will bring in special guests for days he has scheduled performances in Las Vegas and elsewhere. Call the theater to confirm show dates. Admission: $19.95; children under 12, $10.95. The theater is located on Shepherd of the Hills Expressway, one-half mile west of Missouri 248. P.O. Box 1567, Branson, MO 65616. Phone: 417-336-3986.

BREAKING INTO THE BRANSON MUSIC SCENE

With the growth of Branson as a live performance center for country music, droves of performers have come looking for work. Many have been disappointed. Branson shows don't hold any organized, open auditions. When there is an opening, the show owners go to a file of tapes and résumés to call in the most promising for an audition. Theater owners say prospective performers are welcome to send an audio- or video-tape, photograph and résumé. But they say to send material that doesn't have to be returned.

The best shot for breaking into the Branson music scene is to apply to perform on the "That's Showbiz" Talent Show. Every year from the first of November through mid-April, talent scout Tony James hosts Monday night showcases at Tommy's Lounge. The program is in its fourteenth year. One hundred and forty contestants from across the country will have the opportunity to perform a number onstage this year. Many former contestants and winners have gone on to get performance jobs in Branson. The talent show draws a big audience among whom may be theater owners, producers, and agents, some from as far as Los Angeles.

James books his talent contestants more than a year in advance. He'll start booking in August and September for the following season's lineup. Last year more than 300 people applied. And James takes offense if anyone calls this an "amateur show." The contestants are well-seasoned and polished. One recent contestant was a former "Star Search" winner. Contestants who are selected rehearse with James's band the day before the 8 P.M. show.

To apply, call and leave your name and phone number at 417-334-0003. James calls back to talk about your experience, your talent. He'll tell you whether or not to send a tape. Or write to "That's Showbiz," P.O. Box 1793, Branson, MO 65616. Or call Tommy's Lounge, 417-334-4995.

DON'T MISS!! SILVER DOLLAR CITY

In the late 1940s a Chicago-area vacuum-cleaner salesman named Hugo Herschend began bringing his wife Mary and young sons Jack and Peter to visit a tourist attraction called Marvel Cave. In 1949, as a retirement project, Herschend bought the cave. Before his dreamed-of improvements could be realized, Herschend died, and the running of the business was left to Mary and her sons.

The former librarian loved the challenge—and had the vision. To expand the tourist attraction above ground, an 1890s village was designed and opened in 1960. Since then, the park has grown into a colony of 100 authentically-costumed craftspeople, 46 shops, 15 rides, 12 restaurants, and eight live-performance locations.

The Herschend brothers still own the park, along with entertainer Kenny Rogers, and have made sure that attention to detail, authenticity, and friendliness remain the park's trademarks.

DON'T MISS!! Guided tours of Marvel Cave, with the largest entrance room of any cave in America, also remain a popular activity at Silver Dollar City. More than 500 steps leading down into the cave can prohibit some from the tour, but it's a fascinating trek if you're up to it.

Music Shows

Except for the evening performances in Echo Hollow Amphitheater, music shows are held often throughout the park all day long. There also are wandering street performers and plenty of costumed characters. Be sure to have a chat with the City's sheriff. Silver Dollar City offers:

Silver Dollar Saloon: Buffalo Fred brings his Wild West Show to the Saloon for performances throughout the day. The Western Comedy Revue includes everything from trick shooting to the Buffalo Gals tossing their dancing skirts.

Dockside Theater: Traditional Dixieland, ragtime, and lively jazz from the Old South. Also the site of the Backyard Circus, where children are invited to become stars of the show.

Western Music Roundup: Rotating between the Dockside and the Music Gazebo, the entertainment includes Texas swing, yodeling, and the Cajun fiddle music of Wade Benson Landry.

The Music Gazebo: Southern Gospel and bluegrass in the center of the town's park. Relax on the benches and enjoy the sounds.

Valley Theater: Sit for a spell in the shaded hollow and enjoy the folk music roots of today's country music. You'll be entertained by the best "porch musicians" to be found in these hills.

Riverfront Playhouse: The "Riverboat Ramble" is a musical variety trip down the Mississippi River performed throughout the day in this air-conditioned theater.

Echo Hollow Amphitheater: Evening music shows in this 3700-seat outdoor amphitheater after the park closes feature Warner Brothers recording artists, the Branson Brothers. Free to park guests.

Rides

The rides at Silver Dollar City are designed as family fun, even the new "Thunderation" roller coaster. This ride opens April '93. Rising 81 feet amidst the treetops, and reaching a top speed of 48 mph, the roller coaster is designed for comfort and a secure feeling.

Watch out for some rides that can be a drenching experience, including the American Plunge, the Lost River, Fire-in-the-Hole, Lost River of the Ozarks, Shoot Out in the Flooded Mine, and the Wilderness Waterboggan.

For relaxation, ride the Frisco Line Train Ride. The German-built engines and rolling stock winds around on nearly three miles of track through the City.

Be sure the children have time to spend at Tom Sawyer's Landing, where they'll love the balloon ride, the carousel, Ferris wheel, and the "kid-powered" gold-miner's ore carts. More entertainment for the young ones is on tap at the Magical Craft Forest Carousel Barn, where experts help the little ones make a craft they can take home.

DON'T MISS!! Shopping

All the shops in the City offer quality merchandise at surprisingly reasonable prices.

In *Sullivan's Mill and Bakery*, the smells will convince you to try fresh-baked goodies while watching corn and wheat being ground by the water-wheel-driven mill.

Try the *Coin Cutter* for unique jewelry made from intricately sawed coins.

Opal's Doll Orphanage is the perfect place to go if you've got grandchildren, or if you're still a kid at heart.

Mtn. Outfitters Gun and Knife Shop features handmade knives, black-powder rifles, and all the accessories.

Book & Print Shop—a book lover's delight, with many unique volumes.

Ezra's Toys specializes in old-fashioned wooden toys, games, and puzzles. If you're with someone talented, maybe they'll play a tune on an Irish tin whistle for you.

Scrimshaw: You'll find hand engravings on bone and fossil for knives, belt buckles, and jewelry.

There's also the Basket Factory, Brown's Candy Factory, Hillcreek Pottery, Mountain Woodcarvers, Sophie's Strawberry Shop, and Everything Apples Shop.

Many of the shops feature the artists and craftspeople at work on their wares. BARGAIN ALERT!! Check the rear of shops for sales and bargain tables.

Dining

Silver Dollar City's head chef, R. Douglas Zader, who oversees the cooking for the park's dozen restaurants, weighs . . . well, suffice it to say his nickname's "Moose."

And the man sure knows how to cook. From the half-pound cinnamon rolls to the red-beans-and-rice with smoked sausage at Aunt Polly's

Parlor, the food's as good as everything else in the park.

Prices are reasonable, with full meals for one person running from about $4 to $8.

DON'T MISS!! *Mary's Pie and Sandwich Shoppe* for wonderful home-baked pies like chocolate cream, apple, and strawberry-rhubarb.

Hannah's for the biggest chocolate chip cookies ever. Try one with a bowl of homemade, hand-dipped ice cream.

Riverside Ribhouse: A great place for baby-back pork ribs and barbecued smoked chicken.

The Mine: try the bountiful buffet in this homey mine shaft: beef stew, fried chicken, ham and beans, salads and cornbread.

The Lumbercamp Restaurant for burgers, rib-eye sandwich, mesquite chicken breast sandwiches, or a catfish Po'Boy.

Molly's Mill Restaurant: All-you-can-eat buffet breakfast served from 8 A.M.—one hour before the park opens—to 11 A.M. From noon until the park closes, there's more buffet with fried chicken, catfish, vegetables, and salads.

Settler's Ridge Smokehouse: Silver Dollar City's award-winning barbecue sauce adorns baby-back pork ribs, sandwiches, and smoked chicken here.

BUDGET ALERT!! There are early evening dinner specials here from 4 P.M. to park closing.

Granny's Chicken Pantry: Homemade spaghetti and meat sauce is served in a home-baked bread bowl, formed over a bucket.

There are lots of treats available from street vendors too, including chopped apples smothered with warm caramel sauce and nuts, bowls of strawberries and cream, the best funnel cakes in town with a maple cream topping, fresh cider and lemonade, and freshly fried pork rinds.

Special Events, 1993

April 10–25: Flower and Garden Festival, sponsored by *Midwest Living* magazine. This is a blooming extravaganza with thousands of flower displays, gardening tips, and lots of special exhibits.

June 11–20: Silver Dollar City Music Festival. Musicians from across the country, more than 200, come to fiddle, clog, and sing. Family bands and everything from jazz to gospel crop up on every street corner.

August 28–September 12: National Quilt Festival. Quilt lovers can learn new techniques, admire the fancy handiwork, or shop for quilting supplies. More than forty visiting quilters participate.

September 15–October 31: National Crafts Festival. More than 100 visiting crafters come from around America to display, demonstrate, and sell their wares. Special food treats at harvest time too.

November 11–December 19: Old-Time Country Christmas. More than 100 miles of twinkling lights turn the City into a magic kingdom with Christmas songs, food, and a living nativity.

Operating Schedule

March 27 and April 3 . . . 9 A.M. to 6 P.M.
April 10 through May 21
(closed Mondays and Tuesdays) . . . . . .
   9:30 A.M. to 6 P.M.
May 22 through August 22, daily . . . . .
   9:30 A.M. to 7 P.M.
August 23 through October 31, daily . . .
   9:30 A.M. to 6 P.M.
   (Saturdays 9 A.M. to 7 P.M.)
November 11 through December 19 . . .
   noon to 10 P.M.
   (Thursdays through Sundays.
   Closed Thanksgiving.)

Admission

	Adult	Over 55	Children 4–11
One-Day ticket	$22.00	$21.00	$13.00
Season Pass	33.00		23.00
(June 1–			
October 31)			
Christmas,	9.95		5.95
one-day			

Combination tickets with admission to White Water and Silver Dollar City also are available. Enter after 3 P.M., the next day is free.

Tips to Make It Easy

* ★ Allow two days to take in Silver Dollar City's shows and rides as well as a walk through Marvel Cave.
* ★ Arrive early. The park opens for breakfast an hour before the other park attractions. If you can't come early, wait until afternoon. Peak hours for the rides are from noon to 4 P.M. If you arrive early, ride the rides in the morning and see the shows in the afternoon.
* ★ Best days to visit are Thursdays, Fridays, and Sundays, traditionally the days of lower attendance.

★ Wear comfortable clothing and walking shoes. Portions of the park are a little hilly, but still easily accessible to all.

★ Begin your walk through the park by following the streets to the left, past the Wilderness Church. That gets the steepest grades out of the way on the downhill direction.

★ Free trams run from the large parking-lot areas to the entrance. They run until the last guest is shuttled. Parking is free.

★ Admission to the Branson Brothers evening performance in the amphitheater thirty minutes after the park closes is free to day guests.

★ Some guests bring their pets to the park. Dogs are not prohibited, but must be kept on leashes. All food locations will give your pet a cup of water.

★ The park accepts VISA, MasterCard, Discover, and personal checks for the amount of purchase. There also is an automatic teller machine in the ticket booth area.

★ Strollers, wheelchairs, electric carts, and lockers are available to rent.

★ At each ride there is a sign advising what to expect and listing any restrictions, such as height. At most rides guests in wheelchairs must be assisted from the chair onto the ride. Personnel are not trained to do this, and not permitted to assist.

COMING ATTRACTIONS!! The Silver Dollar City development team never takes a vacation. Opening in the spring of 1995, watch for White River Landing. The new attraction on nearby Table Rock Lake will feature a dining and shopping village on shore with a 1000-seat showboat for entertainment on the water.

For information and tickets to Silver Dollar City, write: Silver Dollar City, Branson MO 65616. Phone: 417-338-8210.

SPECIAL ATTRACTIONS

There's plenty to entertain in Branson besides the music shows. There are lots of go-carts, bumper cars, mini-golf courses, and horseback riding stables. Here are a few other attractions to add to your "Things to Do" list. And DON'T MISS!! the special section beginning on page 40 for the Silver Dollar City theme park too.

Elvis-A-Rama: A tribute to Elvis featuring a 110-foot mural depicting scenes of his life, including music and statements recorded by those who knew and loved "The King." The show lasts about 25 minutes, and will be moving for Elvis's fans. Open Mondays through Saturdays with hourly shows from 10 A.M. to 8 P.M., Sundays 10 A.M. to 6 P.M. Admission: $4. In the Branson Mall next to Memory Lane Theater; 417-335-3777.

The Lake Queen and the Sammy Lane Pirate Cruise: The Sammy Lane Boat Line has been in continuous operation on Lake Taneycomo since 1916. The seventy-minute cruise highlights White River history and includes a fight with a pirate. The *Lake Queen* offers breakfast and dinner tours as well as a Fourth of July fireworks cruise. Operates April through October, as weather permits. Admission: sightseeing cruise, $6.95; children 3–12, $4.50; breakfast cruise, $12.95; children 3–12, $7.50; dinner cruise, $16.95; children 3–12, $8.00; children under 3 free. Senior discounts. Address: 280 N. Lake Drive, Branson, MO 65616. Phone: 417-334-3015.

Mutton Hollow Craft and Entertainment Village: This thirty-acre turn-of-the-century village features crafters demonstrating their work, music shows, and an old-time country fair area with a 1930 carousel and a Ferris wheel. The park is open daily beginning March 20. Admission: $8.95; children under 12, $3.95. Just off Missouri 76 at the west end of the strip, near the Ray

Stevens Theatre. P.O. Box 250, Branson, MO 65616. Phone: 417-334-4947.

Ride the Ducks: Try this seventy-minute ride in an amphibious vehicle for the thrill of a splashy entry off the road into Table Rock Lake. It's a chance for a different vantage point—looking back at the shoreline. The tour includes a ride through Shepherd of the Hills Fish Hatchery. Now in its 22nd season, the Ducks open April 1 with tours daily every fifteen minutes from 8 A.M. to 5:30 P.M. as late in the season as weather permits. Located on Missouri 76, 2½ miles west of U.S. 65. Call 417-334-3825. Admission in 1992 was $9.95; children under 12, $4.95.

Shepherd of the Hills Homestead and Outdoor Theater: On the site where Harold Bell Wright wrote his best-selling book in 1907, *The Shepherd of the Hills,* you can take a Jeep-drawn tour and see Old Matt's actual cabin. The park also features craft shops and restaurants, themed with the book's setting, and plenty of activities for the kids, including a petting zoo featuring animals mentioned in the book.

For the past 32 years, the drama has been brought to life in the 1842-seat amphitheater with a cast of 75, horse-drawn wagons, and even the burning cabin. The park opens daily from 9 A.M. to 5:30 P.M. on April 17. Admission to the Homestead: $12.95; children under 12, $6.95.

The pageant is nightly at 8:30 P.M.; 7:30 P.M. after Labor Day. Admission: $14.95; children under 12, $7.95. A combination ticket also is available. On the west end of Missouri 76. Route 1, Box 770, Branson, MO 65616. Call 417-334-4191.

Long's Wax and Historical Museum: In the narrow corridors of this museum, which has been in Branson for 25 years, you'll find hundreds of life-sized figures, including movie stars, historical figures, horror characters, and 100 figures depicting the life of Christ from his birth to the resurrection. Interesting groupings include a figure of Farrah Fawcett in a cubicle beside Gandhi. And there's a row of coffins containing likenesses of Nazi villains, including Hitler and Mussolini; in the next cubicle, the figures of President Ronald Reagan and Oliver North. The museum also features antique cars and taxidermied animals, including a two-headed calf. Open daily from 8:30 A.M. to 11 P.M. Admission: $4; children 6 through 11, $1.50. Address: 3030 Highway 76 West. Phone: 417-334-4145.

White Water: On a hot day this is the place to be. There's fun for all ages and degrees of water confidence at this water park. The Tropical Twister is 500 feet of wet fun. Float in the sun along Paradise River. Don't miss the Wave Pool. Let the little ones have fun on Little Squirt's Island. Or just relax under the palm trees—yes, real ones. You can purchase refreshments at the Tradewinds Cafe or the Beachcomber Deli. Or you can bring your own cooler, but alcohol and glass containers are prohibited.

One Day Admissions:

Ages 12–54	$15.00
Ages 4–11	$11.00
Ages 55+	$5.50

For an afternoon splash, prices after 4 P.M. are $9, $7, and $3 respectively.

Open May 15 and 16, 10 A.M. to 6 P.M. May 22 through August 29, daily, 10 A.M. to 9 P.M. September 4, 5, and 6, 10 A.M. to 6 P.M. Address: 3505 Highway 76 West, Branson, MO 65616. Phone: 417-334-7488.

Ralph Foster Museum: At nearby College of the Ozarks, three miles south of Missouri 76 off U.S. 65, the museum is named for the man who set up KWTO radio station in Springfield, where plenty of country talent got their first break. Porter Wagoner, Chet Atkins, and the Carter Family were among the live radio performers. Foster also produced "Ozark Jubilee," an early television music show starring Red Foley. The museum houses natural history displays, an extensive gun collection, the Beverly Hillbillies car, and a special collection of area resident Rose O'Neill's Kewpie dolls. Closed in January. Open Mondays through Saturdays 9 A.M. to 4 P.M.; Sundays 1 to 4 P.M. Admission: $4; seniors, $3; students, free. College of the Ozarks, Point Lookout, MO 65726. Phone: 417-334-6411, ext. 3407.

SHOPPING

For a break from the music shows, there's plenty of fun places to shop in Branson, including an outlet mall. Unless otherwise noted, these shops are open year-round.

Shops on the strip

Appletree Mall Crafts and Collectibles: This converted supermarket houses a wide variety of handmade crafts, gifts, and craft supplies. Open daily 9 A.M. to 11 P.M. Address: 1830 West Missouri 76. Phone: 417-335-2133.

Branson Mall: Between Wal-Mart and Consumers Market, the mall is a fun place to wander. Live entertainment in the food court adds to the charm of several shops, including Maurices, where you can pick up the latest in western wear; and the Ernest Tubb Record Shop, for the latest country hits as well as old classics. Stop by the Hey Mon Coffee Roastery to buy freshly roasted coffee beans or to try a cup of more than 25 varieties of brew. Inside the Branson Mall also is where you'll find Memory Lane Theater.

DON'T MISS!! *The Engler Block:* More than 25 shops highlight Ozark crafts with lots of working crafters. When Peter Engler renovated this 40,000-square-foot warehouse in 1986, the reproduction of his grandfather's general store was the first project. Engler himself is a widely-known woodcarver. He's collected the best artisans to produce unusual products on the premises, even gingerbread trim custom-made at the Silver Creek Mill for your Victorian house. Other shops include the Ozark Mountain Gem and Clock Shop and White River Metalworks for custom jewelry. January/February hours: 10 A.M. to 5 P.M. March through December, 9 A.M. to 6 P.M. Address: 1335 Highway 76 West, Branson, MO 65616. Phone: 417-335-2200.

DON'T MISS!! *The Grand Village:* Scheduled to open in May '93, this shopping experience was built by Silver Dollar City, Inc., with all the traditional attention to quality and detail. The atmosphere is Old South, with a touch of Charleston and New Orleans. The 22 shops face in toward a cobblestone courtyard decked with flowers. Shop for the perfect hat at Tumbleweeds or that special fuzzy friend at Bear Hollow. Abbey Rose is a shop that looks like a Victorian home. Wander through the dining room or the reading room, and if you see something you like, everything's for sale.

For hungry shoppers, try the soda fountain in the Hard Luck Diner. Reminiscent of the "Happy Days" diner, here you will find an honest-to-goodness soda jerk waiting to make you a strawberry soda. Or try the Village Cafe where you will find several kinds of coffees to go with the tarts, beignets, or other baked goodies. Next to the Grand Palace on Highway 76 West. Open daily in May from 9 A.M. to 9 P.M.; Sundays, 10 A.M. to 6 P.M. June through October, daily from 9 A.M. to 10 P.M.; Sundays, 10 A.M. to 10 P.M. November 1 through 5, daily from 9 A.M. to 6 P.M.; Sundays 10 A.M. to 6 P.M. November 6 through December 23, daily 9 A.M. to 10 P.M.; Sundays, 10 A.M. to 9 P.M. December 26 through March 1, daily from 9 A.M. to 6 P.M.; Sundays, 10 A.M. to 6 P.M. Closed on Easter, Thanksgiving Day, Christmas Day, and New Year's Day. On Missouri 76 next to the Grand Palace. Phone: 417-335-4424.

Outback Outfitters: This fascinating shop has imported clothing for men and women, great exotic jewelry and unusual gifts from around the world. Australian items from toy koala bears to emu-skin wallets are featured. Located next to the

Outback Steak and Oyster Bar at 1914 Highway 76 West. Open daily from 9 A.M. to 9 P.M. Phone: 417-334-7003.

Singing Sensations Recording Studio: Become a recording star! Technicians here will set you up in a private booth where you can practice singing along to any of more than 400 prerecorded sound tracks to favorite songs. Let them know when you're ready, and they'll record the results for $11.95. For an eight-song tape, it's $60.95. Or you can buy the background music tapes for $6.95 if you're preparing to enter a talent contest. And for $24.95, they'll videotape the event too. On Missouri 76 in Stacey's Ozark Village, next to the Moe Bandy Americana Theatre. P.O. Box 1665, Branson, MO 65616. Phone: 417-335-4435; 800-677-4602.

Yeary's Music Stand: On the lower level of the Harbortown Mall on Missouri 76, this remarkable shop has all kinds of items for music buffs, from guitar-shaped earrings and bolo ties to swimsuits with a keyboard pattern up the sides. It also has candies: chocolate guitars and musical note-shaped suckers. Open daily 9 A.M. to 8 P.M. from May through October; 9 A.M. to 6 P.M. November through April. HCR 5, Box 1709-1, Branson, MO 65616. Phone: 417-225-5456; 800-688-1548.

BRANSON

Downtown Branson

In the few blocks it takes to wander the "old" downtown, you'll find ninety interesting shops and a dozen flea markets. Downtown you'll also find practical things like pharmacies and a shoe repair shop as well as bakeries, hometown cafés, and a fudge shop. Here's a few highlights:

Carousel Gift House: Here you'll find a wide array of dolls, including Kewpies and Madame Alexander dolls as well as unusual finds like wooden paper dolls. Also, all kinds of miniatures. Open daily 9 A.M. to 8 P.M. Address: 115 W. Main Street. Phone: 417-334-5655.

DON'T MISS!! *Dick's Oldtime 5 & 10-cent Store:* It's like the place you went when you were a kid; the place where the smells of popcorn and bubble gum, yard goods and Evening in Paris, blended into a new scent; where old wooden floors sagged under the weight of everything you could possibly need or want. This is not a reproduction. It's been open since 1929. And there's a good chance that owner Dick Hartly will wait on you. Open daily 8:30 A.M. to 8 P.M., except on Sundays, from 10 A.M. to 5 P.M. Address: 103 W. Main Street. Phone: 417-334-2410.

The Doll House: The big pink building is home to tons of dolls, including Kewpies, as well as doll houses and furniture. Open daily 9:30 A.M. to

5:30 P.M. Address: 704 S. Commercial. Phone: 417-334-3233.

The Fudge Shop: Homemade treats including brittles and taffy. TIP! This is where you'll find Dolly Parton–shaped chocolate lollipops for 79 cents. They make great souvenirs to take home. Just keep them cool. Open daily 9 A.M. to 6 P.M. Address: 106 South Business 65. Phone: 417-335-8637.

DON'T MISS!! *Mar-Lea's Boutique:* This glitzy shop provides lots of the costumes for Branson performers and has a full array of sequin and bangled wear for wannabes. Open Mondays through Saturdays 9 A.M. to 5:30 P.M. Address: 114 W. Main. Phone: 417-334-8393.

Mountain Music Shop: If you get caught up in mountain dulcimer music, this shop has dulcimers starting at $39. They'll even get you strumming with a free ten-minute lesson. Open daily 9 A.M. to 5 P.M. Address: 109 North Business 65 in downtown Branson. Phone: 417-334-0515.

Patricia's House: Everything with a Victorian look, including wreaths, dolls, hats, lamps, and antique furniture. In the historic old Security Bank of Branson building. Open daily 9 A.M. to 6 P.M. Address: 101 W. Main. Phone: 417-335-8001.

Outlet Mall

Just when you thought it was safe to holster that checkbook . . .

Factory Merchant's Mall: Just north of Missouri 76 on Pat Nash Drive, fifty outlet stores offer bargains on brand-name merchandise. An additional thirty stores are set to open the summer of '93. Outlets include Carter's Childrenswear, Oshkosh B'Gosh, Bon Worth, Bugle Boy, Evan Picone, Geoffrey Beene, Jonathan Logan, Van Heusen, Corning/Revere, Pfaltzgraff, Florsheim, Hush Puppies, and American Tourister. Hours January and February: daily, 10 A.M. to 6 P.M.; March through December, Mondays through Saturdays, 9 A.M. to 8 P.M.; Sundays, 9 A.M. to 6 P.M. Closed Easter, Thanksgiving, and Christmas days. Phone: 417-335-6686.

NEARBY TOWNS AND ACTIVITIES

To get away from the bustle of the strip, you don't have to go far. Lake activities are plentiful, inexpensive, and a cool thing to do on a hot summer day. And there are nearby towns that offer other attractions as well.

Table Rock State Park Marina: Five miles south of Missouri 76 on Missouri 165, you can picnic, camp, or rent all kinds of boats and jet skis. Try parasailing 300 feet above the water! Camping sites are let on a first-come, first-get basis. No reservations. HCR 9, Box 1470, Branson, MO 65616. Phone: 417-334-4704.

Pointe Royale Golf Course: Open to the public. Greens fees and cart rental for 18 holes, $48. For tee times call 417-334-4477. Three miles south of Missouri 76 on Missouri 165. TIP! If you sign up for a Wednesday morning, you may be in fine company. This is when several of Branson's stars get together for a round of relaxation.

Kimberling City: Twelve miles west of Silver Dollar City on Missouri 13, this lakeside town is host to a variety of boating activities, fishing, and cozy lakeside resorts. Table Rock Lake–Kimberling City Chamber of Commerce, P.O. Box 495, Kimberling City, MO 65686. Phone: 417-739-2564.

Reeds Spring: This little town fifteen miles northwest of Silver Dollar City on Missouri 13 was founded in 1871 and has become a haven for artists, craftspeople, and musicians allergic to country music. Here, visitors find quaint shops like Jimonna's Handmade Jewelry and the Old Time Music Emporium. On weekends there's live music at Fernando's Hideaway ranging from folk to jazz. For information about special art events in town:

Reeds Spring Development Association
P.O. Box 372
Reeds Spring, MO 65737
Phone: 417-272-8568; 417-272-3369.

Rockaway Beach: This quiet resort community, nine miles northeast of Branson on Missouri 176 off U.S. 65, was founded in 1917. Its year-round population of 300 annually welcomes a couple of thousand folks who want to stay out of the bustle of Branson. From the banks of Lake Taneycomo, fishing enthusiasts catch brown and rainbow trout. The town boasts several motels, lodges, and resorts with kitchenettes. Along Beach Boulevard several marinas rent boats, provide fishing equipment, and offer guide services. For visitors information:

Rockaway Beach Chamber of Commerce
P.O. Box 1004-P
Rockaway Beach, MO 65740
Phone: 417-561-4280; 800-798-0178

Springfield: Fifty miles north on U.S. 65 is the city that's home to Bass Pro Shops Outdoor World, the world's largest sporting goods store. But it's more than a store. Inside are a four-story waterfall, a fish and wildlife museum, a trout stream, six huge aquariums with fish-feeding shows, Hemingway's Restaurant, and more. Last year, 3.5 million people visited the 150,000-square-foot store at 1935 S. Campbell. Phone: 417-887-1915. For more information on other Springfield attractions:

Springfield Convention and Visitors
   Bureau
3315 E. Battlefield Road
Springfield, MO 65804
Phone: 417-881-5300.

DINING

There's lots of treats in store for Branson diners, and it's in a price range that'll keep your wallet happy. There are plenty of buffet restaurants in the $4.95 to $8.95 range per person for dinners. And there are "special occasion" places too, where two people can have a nice meal with a little wine for under $50.

Restaurants included here take major credit cards, unless otherwise noted, are handicapped accessible, and most are open year-round. There are plenty of other good restaurants not included here, such as the normal array of chains like Shoney's, Bonanza, and Taco Bell.

Adams Rib Restaurant: Moderately priced break-fast, lunch, and dinner with yummy hickory-smoked meats the specialty in this 106-seat restaurant. They do not take credit cards. Open February 26 through mid-December. Daily except Sundays, 7:30 A.M. to 9 P.M. Address: 1645 Highway 76 West, Branson, MO 65616. Phone: 417-334-8163.

Baldknobbers Country Restaurant: This 250-seat buffet and menu-service restaurant opens in March when the Baldknobbers Hillbilly Jamboree begins operations and remains open through December when the show closes. Open daily 6:30 A.M. to 8 P.M. for down-home country cooking. Address: 2843 Highway 76 West. Call 417-334-7202.

Bob Evans Restaurant: This is old-fashioned American vittles. The Daily Bargain on Fridays: pork roast and dressing with all the trimmings, for $5.95. Lots of à la carte vegetables, including turnip greens and bacon. There's live entertainment all day in this 200-seat eatery, and a great gift shop fashioned after an old-time general store. Open Sundays through Thursdays, 6 A.M. to 10 P.M.; weekends, 6 A.M. to 1 A.M. At the junction of U.S. 65 and Missouri 76. Call 417-336-2023.

Branson Cafe: The oldest restaurant in Taney County. In downtown Branson, it's a great place to stop for biscuits and gravy or a piece of home-made pie. Open daily except Sunday, 5:30 A.M. to 8 P.M. Address: 120 W. Main Street. Phone: 417-334-3021.

B.T. Bones Steakhouse: This is a Texas roadhouse atmosphere, casual and fun, with some of the best steaks in town: Iowa choice beef, cut fresh daily. Live music every night, and Killian Red beer on tap. Restaurant seats 200. Prices range from $6.95 for chopped sirloin to $14.95 for an 18-ounce T-bone. Open Mondays through Saturdays from 11 A.M. to 1 A.M.; Sundays, noon to midnight. On Shepherd of the Hills Expressway near the Wayne Newton Theatre. Phone: 417-335-2002.

DON'T MISS!! *Candlestick Inn:* Perched 250 feet atop Mount Branson, overlooking Lake Taneycomo and downtown Branson, the Candlestick offers fine food with a spectacular view. There's a deck for cocktails in the summer. If you come for Ozark Mountain Christmas, be sure to have dinner here for a great view of the lights. Seats 150 with a lounge. Dinners priced from $10.95 to $29.95. The Candlestick, a favorite with area residents for thirty years, is closed the first two weeks in January. Open daily at 4 P.M. Reservations are a good idea. Ask for a window seat. To get there, take U.S. 65 Business south through downtown, across the Lake Taneycomo bridge to Missouri 76 East. Drive along the lakeshore, up the hill, and turn left at the sign. Follow the road straight for a quarter-mile. Phone: 417-334-3633.

DON'T MISS!! *Copper Penny:* This 220-seat restaurant has been a favorite of locals for years. The lounge is cozy and has dart tournaments. The prime rib is among the best around, and the huge dinner salads are spectacular. Prime rib, salad, potato, homemade bread for $14.95. Reservations are a good idea. Address: 1525 Highway 76 West. Phone: 417-334-5097.

DON'T MISS!! *Devil's Pool Restaurant:* At the Big Cedar Lodge, this hunting-lodge-style restaurant features great prime rib and lots of other treats. The Sunday morning brunch is a great way to start the day and then graze for hours. In the fall, grab a table by the fireplace. In summer, look out over Table Rock Lake. Prices range from $8.50 to $19.50 for dinners. Reservations recommended. Take U.S. 65 ten miles south of Branson. Turn east on Missouri 86 and follow the signs. Phone: 417-335-2777.

DON'T MISS!! *Dimitris:* Born in Greece, Dimitrios Tsaharidis wanted to own a restaurant all his life. He has done so in Branson for the past twelve years, and diners looking for gourmet treats and service that equals the best anywhere have enjoyed the benefits. After a fire destroyed his original lakefront restaurant, Dimitris is now located at Roark Vacation Resort, 403 North Business 65 in downtown Branson. He plans to open a floating restaurant near the old location at the end of Main Street on Lake Taneycomo in the spring of 1993. The restaurant will feature an elegant, upscale dining room as well as a family-style restaurant. Dimitrios will be there in his tuxedo to greet you, unless he's fixing his famous Caesar salad tableside. Prices for the dining room range from $9.95 for catfish to $45.95 for Steak Diane for two. Reservations are recommended. Phone: 417-334-0888.

Fall Creek Steakhouse: This 366-seat steakhouse is the home of the "thrown roll." A waiter tosses freshly baked rolls to diners from a large tray. For a treat, they provide sorghum molasses for sopping the rolls. Dinners come with a family-style salad bowl and range from $6.99 to $14.99 for a rack of hickory-smoked ribs. Side orders include fried green tomatoes and baked sweet potatoes. Or try an "Ozark Blossom"—a whole onion cut like a flower, battered and deep-fried. Open Sundays through Thursdays, 11 A.M. to 10 P.M.; Fridays and Saturdays, 11 A.M. to 11 P.M.

Located on Missouri 165, 1½ miles south of Missouri 76. Phone: 417-335-8521.

The Farmhouse Restaurant: In downtown Branson, here's the place to find chicken fried steak and homemade blackberry cobbler. On weekends you can go for breakfast after the show at this 100-seat restaurant. Open Sundays through Thursdays, 7 A.M. to 9:30 P.M.; weekends, 7 A.M. to midnight. At the corner of Missouri 76 and U.S. 65 Business. Phone: 417-334-9701.

Gilley's Texas Cafe: This roomy restaurant serves up Tex-Mex and other treats. DON'T MISS!! Gilley's Bullets: cheese-stuffed, deep-fried jalapeño peppers. Prices range from $5.95 for a giant order of chicken nachos to $14.95 for fajitas for two. Open daily at 11 A.M. The kitchen closes at 8 P.M. but the lounge is open to 1 A.M. Address: 3457 Highway 76 West. Phone: 417-335-2755.

Goldie's Patio Grill: Set to open in May '93, behind the Grand Palace, this 300-seat restaurant features "Gourmet Charburgers" and country entertainment. From noon to 9 P.M., solo acts play onstage in the dining room. After 9 P.M., the Lucky 7, a seven-piece show band, goes on. Open daily 7 A.M. to 1 A.M.; Sundays, 7 A.M. to 8 P.M. Address: 2690 Green Mountain Drive. Phone: 417-336-2800.

Kenny Rogers Roasters: The open-pit roasted chicken featured here is mildly seasoned and delicious. Moderate prices in this 112-seat casual place. Open daily from 11 A.M. to 10 P.M. No credit cards. Address: 1305 Highway 76 West. Phone: 417-335-5791.

Koi Garden Oriental Restaurant: A taste of the Far East, with an indoor goldfish pond, hanging lanterns, ceremonial swords, a rickshaw, even private tea rooms where diners remove their shoes and sit on floor cushions. And by the way, they have an extensive menu too. Dinner prices range from $5 to $14. Open Mondays through Saturdays, 11 A.M. to 9 P.M.; Sundays, 11 A.M. to 8 P.M. Next to Bob Evans at the junction of U.S. 65 and Missouri 76. Phone: 417-334-0687.

Mamasita's: Good Mexican food at reasonable prices downtown near the lakefront. This 125-seat restaurant features handmade tortillas, spicy homemade salsa, and an extensive lunch and dinner menu priced from $5.75 to $6.75 for a meal that includes rice and beans. The lounge serves four Mexican brands of beer along with standard domestics, and José Cuervo margaritas. Open daily 11 A.M. to 9 P.M. The lounge stays open until 12:30 A.M. Address: 305 Main Street. Phone: 417-336-6040.

DON'T MISS!! *McGuffey's:* Andy Williams built this restaurant next door to his theater and even provided his own recipe for "Moon River Pasta": marinated broiled tuna with penne noodles sauteed in olive oil, with asparagus tips, for $11.99. Everything's good here. If you like spirits, try an Orangutang: Tang with rum, vodka, and Everclear. Reservations not accepted, and sometimes it can be crowded before and after Andy's shows. TIP! Check in the lounge for seating. They serve the full menu there too. Open Mondays through Saturdays, 11 A.M. to 1:30 A.M.; Sundays, 11 A.M. to midnight. Address: 2600 Highway 76 West. Phone: 417-336-3600.

Mel's Restaurant: Next to the Mel Tillis Theatre, try the yummy buffet for dinner before attending Mel's show. Lots of variety, and tasty too. Also serving breakfast and lunch. After a show, visit the *Mole Hole Ballroom* below the restaurant for dancing to a lively country band. Keep an eye out for Mel. Open daily 6 A.M. to 8 P.M. Lounge open until 1 A.M. U.S. 65 at Missouri 248. Phone: 417-335-5410.

BUDGET ALERT!! *Mr. G's Chicago Style Pizza and Italian Food:* For great pizza in a red-check-ered-tablecloth atmosphere, try this 48-seat diner downtown. They make their own dough and sauce and stuff their own Italian sausage. Try the individual pizza with two toppings for $2.95. Pasta dishes too. Open daily 11 A.M. to 1

P.M. Address: 202 N. Commercial Street, Branson, MO 65616. Phone: 417-335-8156.

BUDGET ALERT!! *Old Apple Mill Restaurant:* The specialty here is the "Family Feast." For $8.50 per adult, $3.95 for children 7–12, you get freshly baked bread, apple muffins, cinnamon rolls, a bowl of salad, mashed potatoes and gravy, corn on the cob, ham and beans, and a family-sized platter of buttermilk-marinated chicken, hickory-smoked ribs, and sliced roast beef. A similar all-you-can-eat breakfast is served for $4.95 for adults, $1.95 for kids 8 and under. Closed from Christmas through mid-March. Open daily 7 A.M. to 9 P.M.; to 10 P.M. during peak season. Address: 3009 Highway 76 West. Phone: 417-334-6090.

DON'T MISS!! *Outback Steak and Oyster Bar:* You'll feel like you went to Australia instead of Branson in this fun place. The decor, all collected during trips down under, is fun to view, and the food—especially the lamb chops and spinach salad with warm bacon dressing—is superb. Dinner prices range from $8.95 to $15.95. It's a great place for lunch too, and has a cozy oyster bar. Reservations recommended. Open daily 11 A.M. till whenever everyone's gone. Address: 1914 Highway 76 West. Phone: 417-334-6306.

Ozark Family Restaurant and Down Under Lounge:
Serving buffets at breakfast, lunch, and dinner,
as well as menu service, with dinners ranging
from $5.99 to $10.95 for a sirloin steak. Open
daily from 7 A.M. to 9 P.M. For rock 'n' roll fans,
check the Down Under Lounge, with live bands
nightly, a dance floor, and pool tables downstairs
below the restaurant. Address: 1580 Highway 76
West. Phone: 417-334-1207.

Pass The Biscuits: Bring your appetite to the
breakfast buffet here. You won't be disappointed. Remember, food has no calories while
you're on vacation! Breakfast buffet with all the
trimmings, $4.25; children ages 3 to 10, $2.95.
Open daily 7 A.M. to 9 P.M. Located at Days Inn,
3524 Keeter Street. Phone: 417-335-8534.

Peppercorns: This 450-seat Victorian-style restaurant across from the Andy Williams Moon River
Theatre features breakfast, lunch, and dinner
buffets in addition to a menu ranging from a
prime rib dinner for $10.95 to lobster tail with all
the trimmings for $19.95. Breakfast buffet is
$4.49; lunch, $5.99; dinner, $8.99. Open daily 7
A.M. to 9 P.M. Address: 2421 Highway 76 West.
Phone: 417-335-6699.

The Plantation: The hefty buffet is the feature in
this 320-seat restaurant. Whether it's breakfast,
lunch, or dinner—which features five meats

from which to choose—you won't go away hungry. Dinner ranges from $7.99 to $12.99. Next to Boxcar Willie's Theatre at 3460 Highway 76 West. Phone: 417-334-7800.

Presley's Juke Box Cafe: Dine in atmosphere reflecting the bebop music of the fifties and sixties. Buffet food at reasonable prices. The restaurant's opening coincides with the seasonal start of Presley's Mountain Music Jubilee in February. No credit cards. Address: 2910 Highway 76 West. Phone: 417-334-3006.

Pzazz Restaurant: This buffet and menu restaurant is at Pointe Royale, a housing development and golf course where many of Branson's stars live. Keep your eyes open for Jim Owen, Andy Williams, Glen Campbell, or Moe Bandy on their way to the links. Open daily 10:30 A.M. to 12:30 P.M. To watch or take part in some classic country two-stepping to a lively band, try the lounge downstairs. Four miles south of Missouri 76 on Missouri 165. Phone: 417-335-2798.

DON'T MISS!! *Rocky's Italian Restaurant:* In downtown Branson, here's a special place. A favorite of year-round residents, the pasta here's a treat, and the bartender knows how to make a dry martini. Moderately priced. Live entertainment, often a jazz combo, on weekends. Serving meals daily except Sundays, from 11 A.M. to 9

P.M. The lounge is open until 1 A.M. and they serve appetizers and sandwiches until midnight. Address: 120 N. Sycamore Street. Phone: 417-335-4765.

Sadie's Sideboard: Next door to the Palace Inn at 2820 Highway 76 West, here's a place to feast at all-you-can-eat buffets for breakfast, lunch, or dinner. Breakfast buffet is $4.45. Also offers full menu service, including fried chicken and cat-fish. Open Mondays through Saturdays, 7 A.M. to 1:30 P.M., 4 to 9 P.M.; Sundays, 7 A.M. to 2 P.M., 4 to 9 P.M. Phone: 417-334-3619.

The Shack Cafe: This is one of those special little places where the local political experts gather in the morning to discuss solutions to the world's problems. Good home cooking too. No credit cards. Open daily except Sundays, 6 A.M. to 8:30 P.M. A cozy, 100-seater downtown at 108 S. Commercial Street. Phone: 417-335-6855.

Starvin Marvin's Family Restaurant: Buffet or menu service in this 100-seat restaurant. Lots of food for a reasonable price. Try the breakfast buffet with all the trimmings for $2.99; children 3–10, $1.99. The dinner specialties are sweet and sour chicken, and hickory-smoked pork ribs. Open daily 7 A.M. to 10 P.M. Address: 3336 Highway 76 West. Phone: 417-334-7402.

DON'T MISS!! *Sugar Hill Farms:* This sunny restaurant features delicious home-baked treats and an eclectic menu. After the meal, check the gift shop and cannery, where you can watch pickles and jams being made. Dinners from $6.95 for pasta to $12.95 for prime rib. Try the Cobb salad: minced lettuce, turkey, bacon, avocado, tomatoes, scallions, and egg for $5.25. Open daily 7 A.M. to 9 P.M. On Missouri 165, one-fifth mile south of Missouri 76. The restaurant closes in January. Phone: 417-335-3608.

Uncle Joe's Bar-b-Q: The motto here is, "You'll wa'na lick your fingers right down to your toes!" Specializing in smoked meats and broiled chicken, this 225-seat restaurant is open daily for lunch and dinner from 11 A.M. to 10 P.M. Address: 2819 Highway 76 West. Phone: 417-334-4548.

DON'T MISS!! BUDGET ALERT!! *Windy City Dogs:* This is a double alert. It's inexpensive and one of those out-of-the-way places lots of visitors miss. It's at the downtown Taneycomo lakefront. Recommendation: order the Chicago-style hot dog—a beef wiener with jalapeño peppers and a dill pickle spear on the bun. You can request fried onions on it too. Get your order "to go" and carry it a half block to the lakefront, where you can sit on a bench, watch the *Lake Queen* paddle wheeler go by, and feed any leftover crumbs to the ducks and geese. Open 11 A.M. to 5 P.M. Address: 315 East Main. Phone: 417-335-3748.

CALENDAR OF AREA EVENTS, 1993

Here's a calendar of some of the area's special events. Towns listed are within a twenty-mile radius of Branson. Phone numbers are included for specific details on the events. For more information, contact the Branson/Lakes Area Chamber of Commerce, P.O. Box 220, Branson, MO 65616. Phone: 900-884-2726.

March

March 1 through May 1: Branson Country Spring. The kickoff event for this celebration is "Branson Jam." This three-day festival features three-hour concerts each day at the Grand Palace, with previews of the upcoming season's music shows. Call the Branson/Lakes Area Chamber of Commerce for more details.

Arts, crafts, musicians' wares, and food from area restaurants will be available under tents in the parking lot. Also, lots of Branson stars will be on hand to have their photo taken and sign autographs. This is Branson's version of Nashville's "Fan Fair."

March 1 through May 14: White Bass Round-Up, Bull Shoals Lake, Forsyth. Phone: 417-546-2741.

March 25–28: Bass Pro Shops' Spring Fishing Classic. This annual tournament brings in the best professional anglers from across the country. More than 100,000 visitors are expected. There are displays and sales of the latest innovations in fishing gear as well as seminars. The indoor events take place at Bass Pro's Outdoor World showroom in Springfield, Missouri, fifty miles north of Branson. For more information, call 417-887-1915, ext. 4330.

March 27–28: Pro-Celebrity Fish-Off in Branson. See professionals and celebrities bring in the fish on Table Rock Lake. Phone: 417-334-4136.

April

April 3–24: Forsyth Art Guild Fine Arts Show, Forsyth. Visitors from all over show their wares at the Taney County seat. Phone: 417-546-2741.

Mid-April, depending on the weather and when the spring foliage blooms: Dogwood Tour Drive, Forsyth. Phone: 417-546-2741.

April 15–18: Kewpiesta in Branson. A celebration of artist and illustrator Rose O'Neill, who created the much-beloved Kewpie doll. Rose spent much of her life in her Taney County home, Bonniebrook, and it was here, in 1912, that she created the doll.

A special celebration in 1993 marks the 100th anniversary of Rose's arrival in the Ozarks. Her restored home is open for tours. Phone: 417-334-3273.

April 23–24: Shriners International Buddy Bass Tournament, Kimberling City. Phone: 417-739-2564.

April 24: Downtown Retailers Spring Cleaning Sidewalk Sale. Phone: 417-334-1548.

May

May 1–22: Forsyth Art Guild Spring China Show. Phone: 417-546-5439.

May 1: Wal-Mart Muscular Dystrophy Association Fishing Tournament, Kimberling City. Phone: 417-739-2564.

May 13–15: State of the Ozarks Fiddlers Convention, Branson. Lots of fiddlin' around. Phone: 417-338-2911.

May 20–22: 13th Annual Spring Craft Festival. Downtown Branson hosts craftspeople from across the country. Phone: 417-334-1548.

June

June 12: Antique Tractor and Engine Show, Shell Knob. Phone: 417-739-2564.

June 12–13: Oink Lawn Downs Pig Races and Barbecue, Cape Fair. Good ol' down-home Ozarks town fair. Phone: 417-739-2564.

June 18–19: Summer Sidewalk Craft Fair, Branson. Phone: 417-334-1548.

June 19–20: Craft Fair, Rockaway Beach. Two days of crafts and fun in this quaint resort town. Phone: 417-561-4280.

July

July 4: Fireworks and parades in Hollister, Kimberling City, Cape Fair, and Shell Knob.

July 14–17: Taney County Fair, Forsyth. Phone: 417-546-2741.

August

August 21: 6th Annual Old-Time Fiddlers Contest, Branson. Fiddlin' and fun by the shores of Lake Taneycomo. Phone: 417-334-1548.

August 26–28: Lions Club Rodeo, Forsyth. Horsing around encouraged. Phone: 417-546-2741.

September

September 10–11: Square Dance Weekend at Compton Ridge Campground, Branson. Phone: 417-338-2911.

September 18–October 30: Shepherd of the Hills Fall Harvest Festival, Branson. Extra old-time crafts and special cooking. Phone: 417-334-4191.

September 23–25: 20th Annual Autumn Daze Craft Festival, Branson. Phone: 417-334-1548.

September 24–25: Harvest Moon Fall Festival, Forsyth. Phone: 415-546-2741.

October

October 1–20: Ozark Country Fall Foliage Drive, Forsyth area. Guided tours of colorful backroads. Phone: 417-546-2741.

October 2–3: White River Gem and Mineral Show, Forsyth. Phone: 417-546-2741.

October 9: Oktoberfest, Kimberling City. Bavaria in the Ozarks. Phone: 417-739-2564.

October 16: Hillbilly Daze Celebration, Hollister. Crafts, food, and fun with a country flair. Phone: 417-334-3050.

November & December— Ozark Mountain Christmas

This celebration, now in its sixth year, has extended Branson's season and brings nearly a half-million visitors to town. This is the time when you'll find more stars than ever in town because Country Music Boulevard is lit with 265 five-foot-diameter stars hung from the lamp posts.

Theaters, restaurants, shops, and motels participate in a decoration extravaganza and special events. Christmas shows at the theaters and special bargains in the shops and outlet mall can put anyone in a festive mood.

The Festival of Lights turns on the second week of November, and the 45th Annual Branson Adoration Parade is held the first Sunday in December.

This special evening parade features dozens of marching bands and lighted floats. During the parade, the Adoration Scene is lit atop Mount Branson. Its forty-foot-tall nativity scene figures can be seen for miles. In 1992 an estimated 35,000 people attended the parade and lighting.

Shepherd of the Hills Homestead and Outdoor Theater offers special evening productions of *The Newborn King*, and the amphitheater is transformed into a scene from Palestine.

And Silver Dollar City outshines itself with more than a hundred miles of lights. The park is open from noon to ten P.M., with characters from Dickens's *Christmas Carol* adding to the special crafts, food, and music.

November 13–14: Shoppers Paradise Holiday Open House, downtown Branson. Phone: 417-334-1548.

December 4: Christmas Parade, Kimberling City. Phone: 417-739-2564. Also, Reeds Spring Christmas Parade, Reeds Spring. Phone: 417-739-2564.

December 5: Branson Adoration Parade and Lighting Ceremony, Branson. Phone: 417-334-4136.

December 11: Forsyth Christmas Parade. Phone: 417-546-2741. Also, Rockaway Beach Christmas Parade and Christmas Countdown Fair, Rockaway Beach. Phone: 417-561-4280.

December 12: Christmas Benefit Music Show, Branson. This three-hour program to raise money for the Chamber of Commerce brings out many of Branson's stars to perform together on-stage. A rare opportunity to sample many of the shows in one place. Phone: 417-334-4136.

LODGING

TIP! Although more than 17,000 lodging rooms provide places for visitors to rest their heads and dream of country music, it's essential to make advance reservations if you want to stay in the motels closest to the music shows along Missouri 76, especially if you plan to visit during the peak tourist season months of May through October.

Most of the motels listed here are along the five-mile strip of Missouri 76, with theaters and restaurants within walking distance. Or catch the Branson trolley, which stops at most motels. (See details in *Getting Around* on page 14.)

There are lots of nice motels and lake resorts off the strip too. If you don't mind driving a couple of miles to theaters, there are some charming lodging places in downtown Branson. Some are listed here.

And to get a little farther out of town—still within a five-mile radius, you can check out the Bed & Breakfast houses, resorts, condos, and campgrounds. Here are a few general tips:

★ Rates listed are for the 1993 season, but BE SURE TO DOUBLE-CHECK RATES WHEN YOU CALL FOR RESERVATIONS.

★ Rates are subject to change and can fluctuate depending on the time of year and day of week. Generally, rates are lower on weekends.

★ BUDGET ALERT!! Off-season rates run from November through March—and April at some places. It could mean as much as a $40 difference in the price of a room. The Ozark Mountain Christmas celebration in November and December is a lovely time to catch the shows, and most motels are down to mid-range or off-season rates. The same goes for the Branson Country Spring festivities March through April.

★ Most lodgings require at least a seven-

day advance notice of cancellation to re-
ceive a deposit refund.

★ All listings include cable TV and in-room
telephones.

★ Open year-round unless otherwise
noted.

★ Approved for major credit cards including Visa, MasterCard, Discover, and
American Express.

★ Unless noted, motels do not accept
pets. Some may take small pets, if you
wheedle.

★ Unless otherwise noted, rooms are
available to accommodate disabled
guests.

★ Rates listed here do not include state
sales tax of 6.7 percent. A two percent
motel tax may be added in 1993.

TIP! For one-stop reservations, The Branson/
Lakes Area Chamber of Commerce offers *Lodging Locator*, a computerized referral service by
telephone. Each motel listed updates its vacan-
cies daily. If you call Mondays through Fridays
from 8 A.M. to 4:30 P.M., an operator will help you
make reservations. After-hours and weekends,
the service is automated and can be used with a
touch-tone phone. To reach the service, call 417-
336-4466.

Hotels/Motels

Alpenrose Inn: This new 50-unit motel has an outdoor pool and offers complimentary continental breakfasts in a dining area. Two people, $59. Children under age 5 stay free. At 2875 Green Mountain Drive, it provides easy access to the Grand Palace and the Andy Williams Moon River Theatre. Phone: 417-336-4600; 800-324-9494.

Amber Light Inn: Next to the Outback Steak and Oyster Bar, this 60-unit motel sits 500 feet off the strip down a tree-lined drive. Outdoor pool. Two people, $32 to $48. P.O. Box 177, Branson, MO 65616. Phone: 417-334-7200; 800-562-0622.

America's Inn 4 Less: This 23-unit motel has an outdoor pool, offers smoking and nonsmoking rooms and free coffee in the morning. Two people, $46.95. Address: 1031 C Highway 76 West, Branson, MO 65616. Phone: 417-334-7380.

Atrium Inn: This 62-unit motel offers an outdoor pool, complimentary continental breakfast, a gift shop, and an ice cream shop and sandwich deli. There are eight units with in-room Jacuzzis. Two people, $59 to $85. Address: 3005 Green Mountain Drive. Phone: 417-336-6000.

Baldknobbers Motor Inn: Within walking distance to nine shows, this 75-unit motel has an outdoor pool, laundry room, and is next to Baldknobbers Country Restaurant. Six rooms available with Jacuzzis for $10 extra. Two people, $47.85 to $58.85. Closed mid-December through February. Address: 2845 Highway 76 West, Branson, MO 65616. Phone: 417-334-7948.

Ben's Wishing Well Motel: Across from Presley's Mountain Music Jubilee, this 150-unit motel has an outdoor pool and offers cable TV with Showtime. Two people, $28 to $54.50. Address: 2935 Highway 76 West, Branson, MO 65616. Phone: 417-334-6950; 800-641-4344.

Best Inns of America: This 66-unit motel is close to the corner of Missouri 165 and Green Mountain Drive in Thousand Hills, with easy access to several theaters, including the Grand Palace. Outside pool and complimentary continental breakfast served in the lobby. Two people, $33 to $78. Address: 3150 Green Mountain Drive, Branson, MO 65616. Phone: 417-336-2378; national reservations, 800-237-8466.

Best Western Branson Inn: On a hilltop next to the Mel Tillis Theatre, at the north edge of Branson on Missouri 65, this 206-room motel offers a great view. Outdoor pool, kiddie pool, and hot tub. Mel's Restaurant and Mole Hole Lounge are at the Inn. Guest laundry room. Two people,

$42.00 to $66.00. P.O. Box 676, Branson, MO 65616. Phone: 417-334-5121; 800-528-1234.

Best Western Knight's Inn: Queen, king or double long-boy beds. Indoor pool and whirlpool. Exercise room. Remote control TVs in all 166 rooms. Guest laundry room. Next to Country Kitchen Restaurant and Lounge. Closed January through mid-February. Two people, $47.75 to $70.75. Address: 3215 Highway 76 West, Branson, MO 65616. Phone: 417-334-1894; 800-528-1234.

Blue Bayou Motor Inn: Close to Roy Clark's Celebrity Theatre, this 73-unit motel features two outdoor swimming pools and an indoor one too. Closed December 20 to March 23. Two people, $36.95 to $65.95. HCR 1, Box 704-20, Branson, MO 65616. Phone: 417-334-5758; outside Missouri, 800-633-3789.

Brighton Place Motel: This 80-unit motel has an outdoor pool and offers complimentary coffee in the lobby. Closed mid-December to March 1. Two people, $39.50 to $55. Small pets are accepted. Address: 3514 Highway 76 West. Phone: 417-334-5510; 800-435-7144.

Comfort Inn: In the Thousand Hills development behind the Grand Palace, this 107-room motel offers an indoor pool, whirlpool and sauna, exercise and game rooms, and guest laundry. Easy access to theaters and restaurants. Two people,

$46 to $88. Closed December 20 to March 12. Address: 203 S. Wildwood Drive, Branson, MO 65616. Phone: 417-335-4727; 800-221-2222.

Compton Ridge Lodge: On Missouri 265, with free shuttle service to Silver Dollar City a mile away, this 30-unit motel and 233-site campground offers indoor and outdoor pools, tennis courts, hiking trails, laundry room, game room, groceries, and church services. Closed mid-December until April 1. Two people, 1992 rates, $42 to $67. HCR 9, Box 1180, Branson, MO 65616. Phone: 417-338-2949; 800-233-8648.

Days Inn: Within four blocks of ten music shows, guests at this 425-room motel enjoy an outdoor pool and Jacuzzi, lighted tennis court, and complimentary continental breakfast. Next to Pass the Biscuits Restaurant. Smoking and nonsmoking rooms. Closed January and February. Two people, $45 to $85. Address: 3524 Keeter Street, Branson, MO 65616. Phone: 417-334-5544; national reservations, 800-325-2525.

Deer Run Motel: On Indian Point Road, 200 yards from Silver Dollar City, this 94-unit motel offers an outdoor pool, game room, Laundromat, and grocery store. Rooms available with kitchenettes. Two people, $55. HCR 1, Box 1168, Branson, MO 65616. Phone: 417-338-2222.

Dutch Kountry Inn: This 150-unit motel next to Peppercorn's Restaurant offers an outdoor pool and three outdoor hot tubs. An additional 140 units are planned for May '93. Free coffee in the lobby. And there are four units with in-room Jacuzzis. Two people, $44.50 to $64.50. Address: 2425 Highway 76 West. Phone: 417-335-2100.

Edgewood Motel: With solid oak furnishings hand-crafted at Silver Dollar City's Furniture Factory, these 217 units are extra-attractive. Extras include an outdoor pool and guest laundry facility. Two people, $34.50 to $69.50. P.O. Box DD, Branson, MO 65616. Phone: 417-334-1000; 800-641-4106.

Gazebo Inn: This 72-unit motel beside the Andy Williams Moon River Theatre is smoke-free. An additional $50 clean-up charge is levied if you smoke. Enjoy the outdoor pool and free morning coffee. Closed December 20 to February 1. Two people, $39.95 to $69.95. Address: 2430 Highway 76 West, Branson, MO 65616. Phone: 417-335-3826; 800-873-7990.

Good Shepherd Inn: This pleasant 39-unit motel has an outdoor pool and provides free coffee in the morning. Located close to Bob Evans Restaurant. Two people, $36.95 to $58.95. Address: 1023 Highway 76 West, Branson, MO 65616. Phone: 417-334-1695; 800-572-7527.

Holiday Inn of Branson: This 220-unit motel, located midway on the strip and across from the Engler Block, features an outdoor pool and Confetti's Restaurant. Live bands and dancing in the lounge. Two people, $52.50 to $100. P.O. Box 340, Branson, MO 65616. Phone: 417-335-5101; 800-465-4329.

Holiday Inn Crowne Plaza: This 501-room, ten-story hotel is set to open September '93, conveniently located between the Grand Palace and the Andy Williams Moon River Theatre. It will offer indoor and outdoor pools, a sauna and workout rooms, suites with kitchens, gift shops, a beauty salon, and a restaurant and lounge operated by McGuffey's restaurants. Prices have not been set. For reservations and information, call the Holiday Inn nationwide number: 800-465-4329.

Lodge of the Ozarks: A classy, 191-room hotel with an indoor pool and hot tub, three gift shops, a styling salon. Try the Rafter's Restaurant for breakfast, lunch, and dinner. Adjoins Roy Clark's Celebrity Theatre. Eighty units have in-room Jacuzzis. Two people, $80 to $95. Address: 3431 Highway 76 West, Branson, MO 65616. Phone: 417-334-7535.

Magnolia Inn: This 152-room motel is on Shepherd of the Hills Expressway, close to Shoji

Tabuchi Theatre, the Ray Stevens Theatre, and the Ozark Mountain Amphitheater. In addition to the outdoor pool, there's a guest laundry and beauty shop. Rooms are available with whirlpool tubs. Two people, $49 to $64. HCR 1, Box 758, Branson, MO 65616. Phone: 417-334-2300; 800-222-7239.

Melody Lane Inn: Located across the strip from the Grand Palace and the Andy Williams Moon River Theatre, this 140-unit motel offers an outdoor swimming pool and hot tub, a laundry room, and a coffee shop for light breakfasts. Closed December 20 to March 1. Two people, $45 to $69. P.O. Box 637, Branson, MO 65616. Phone: 417-334-8598; 800-338-8598.

Mountain Music Inn: Two blocks behind the Cristy Lane Theatre, this 140-unit motel has indoor and outdoor pools and a weight room. If the pools don't please you, it's a short walk to White Water. Two people, $55 to $65. Address: 300 Schaefer Drive, Branson, MO 65616. Phone: 800-888-6933.

Music Country Motor Inn: Near the Baldknobbers Hillbilly Jamboree and Sadie's Sideboard restaurant, this 113-room motel features an outdoor *guitar-shaped* swimming pool! Closed mid-December until mid-March. Two people, $49 to

$57. P.O. Box 236, Branson, MO 65616. Phone: 417-334-1194; 800-826-0368.

Ozark Mountain Inn: A pool, two hot tubs, and a sauna inside a five-story atrium makes this place special. Rooms available with two-person Jacuzzis and water beds. Outdoor pool too. Two people, $65 to $95. Closed December 20 to March 20. Address: 1415 Highway 76 West, Drawer CC, Branson, MO 65616. Phone: 417-334-8300; 800-732-6664.

Palace Inn: TIP! *Stay where George and Barbara Bush stayed during their 1992 campaign visit to Branson—Room 517, marked with a brass plaque.* This 100-room hotel beside the Grand Palace features an outdoor pool and spa, laundry, game room, and breakfast coffee shop. Sadie's Sideboard restaurant is next door. Two people, $47 to $80. Address: 2820 Highway 76 West. P.O. Box 6004, Branson, MO 65616. Phone: 417-334-7666; 800-725-2236.

Quality Inn/Country Music Inn: This 80-unit motel on Green Mountain Drive near Missouri 165 allows easy access to several music shows. They offer an outdoor pool and hot tub and complimentary continental breakfast in the Hearth Room. Two people, $49.95 to $74. Address: 3060 Green Mountain Drive, Branson, MO 65616. Phone: 417-336-3300; 800-364-6874.

Queen Anne Motel I and II: Motel I is 40 units located on Missouri 76 across from White Water. The second location with 88 units is on Schaefer Drive behind the Cristy Lane Theatre. Both locations offer outdoor swimming pools equipped with lifts for use by those with disabilities. Both also offer free coffee and fresh fruit in the mornings. Two people, $39 to $75. P.O. Box 1547, Branson, MO 65616. Phone: 417-335-8100.

Roark Vacation Resort: On Roark Creek in downtown Branson, this time-share condo development also has a 47-unit motel which offers indoor and outdoor pools, sauna, and hot tubs. There is a dock where pontoon boats are available to rent, as well as a restaurant. Two people, $49 to $79. Address: 403 Highway 65 North Business, Branson, MO 65616. Phone: 417-334-3196.

Rustic Oak Motor Inn: Close to downtown, this 109-unit motel features an indoor pool, hot tub and sauna, plus a game room and laundry. Next door to the Rustic Oak Restaurant. Two people, $36 to $64.50. Address: 403 W. Main Street, Branson, MO 65616. Phone: 417-334-6464; 800-828-0404.

76 Mall Inn: This 97-unit motel is in 76 Music Hall complex, where you can see four shows a day. The mall includes Bonanza Family Restaurant, a 36-hole indoor mini-golf course, the 3-D Cinema, a video arcade, and a ton of shops. Or enjoy the outdoor pool and Jacuzzi. Two people, $42 to $65. Address: 1945 76 Highway West, Branson MO 65616. Phone: 417-334-5626; 800-828-9069.

Scottish Inns: One-half mile south of Missouri 76 on Missouri 165, this 62-unit motel has an outdoor pool. Good location for access to alternate routes around the strip at rush hour. Kitchenettes available. Two people, $37.95 to $57.95. HCR 8, Box 280, Branson, MO 65616. Phone: 417-334-5555; 800-782-1620.

Shadowbrook Motel: Sharing 25 acres with the Edgewood Motel, the wooded atmosphere surrounding these 60 units is pleasant for an evening stroll. Outdoor pool and larger-than-average rooms. Not fully equipped to accommodate disabled visitors. Closed mid-December through mid-March. Next to the Home Cannery Family Restaurant. Two people, $42.50 to $80.50. Address: 1810 Highway 76 West. P.O. Box 1127, Branson, MO 65616. Phone: 417-334-4173; 800-641-4600.

Southern Oaks Inn: Located on Shepherd of the Hills Expressway, across from the Shoji Tabuchi Theatre, this 64-unit motel offers an outdoor pool, gift shop, and laundry room. Another 80 units plus an indoor pool and spa are scheduled to be ready in May '93. Two people, 1992 rates, $43.95 to $56.95. HCR 1, Box 759, Branson, MO 65616. Phone: 417-335-8108.

Super 8 Motel: This 73-unit motel is conveniently located behind the Grand Palace and the Andy Williams Moon River Theatre. There is an outdoor pool, and nonsmoking rooms are available; 1993 rates unavailable. Address: 2490 Green Mountain Drive, Branson, MO 65616. Phone: 417-334-8880; 800-800-8000.

Thunderbird Motor Inn: Located next to the Moe Bandy Americana Theatre, this 124-unit motel has an outdoor pool and offers complimentary morning coffee. Two people, $51 to $67. P.O. Box 8, Branson, MO 65616. Phone: 417-334-7771; 800-627-7551.

Victorian Inn: Next to the Boxcar Willie theatre and the Plantation restaurant, this 38-unit motel has an outdoor pool and offers free coffee. Two people, $32.95 to $52.95. Address: 3500 Highway 76 West, Branson, MO 65616. Phone: 417-334-1711.

Ye English Hotel: In downtown Hollister, just across Lake Taneycomo from Branson, you'll find Downing Street, fashioned after an old English village. Many quaint antique shops line the street. The lovely old hotel was built in the early

1920s. The 22 fully-modernized rooms with baths offer an old-world feel. Downstairs is a restaurant and lounge. There also is an outdoor pool. Not equipped to accommodate disabled guests: there is no elevator to second- and third-floor rooms. Two people, $35 to $50. Closed from mid-November to April 1. P.O. Box 506, Branson, MO 65616. Phone: 417-334-4142.

Bed & Breakfasts

To get away from the bustle of the Branson strip, try a stay in one of these homes away from home. In scenic locations, just far enough off the beaten path to give visitors a feel for the Ozarks' abundant natural beauty, they're close enough for convenience. At least a continental breakfast is included in the lodging price. Many serve more hearty fare. Unless otherwise noted, these facilities:

* do not allow smoking in the house
* do not allow pets
* while not encouraged, many allow children over six years old
* accept major credit cards
* require reservations early in the year and have a one-to-two-week advance notice of cancellation for a deposit return

★ are not fully equipped to accommodate visitors with disabilities. Most have rooms at ground level and doorways wide enough to accommodate a wheelchair, but many do not have bathroom rails.

To locate other Bed & Breakfast accommodations within a fifteen-mile radius of Branson, contact Ozark Mountain Country Bed & Breakfast, Box 295, Branson, MO 65616. Phone: 800-695-1546.

Aunt Sadie's Garden Glade: This antique-filled B & B is two miles north of Missouri 76, just off U.S. 65. Units include a garden cottage and two in-house rooms. Outside, there's a hot tub. Smoking is allowed in the cottage and the kitchen only. No pets, but children are allowed. Two people, $65 to $85. Open all year. HCR 7, Box 455, Branson, MO 65616. Phone: 417-335-4063.

The Branson Hotel: This historic landmark in downtown Branson was built in 1903 by the Branson Town Company with the coming of the first railroad. Author of *Shepherd of the Hills*, Harold Bell Wright, stayed here while writing the novel. The hotel also housed the town's first library. Nine guest rooms with private baths range from $75 to $95. Start the morning with complimentary breakfast in the glass-enclosed Breakfast Room and end with a glass of sherry in the Parlour. Open March through December. Address: 214 West Main Street, Branson, MO 65616. Phone: 417-335-6104.

The Brass Swan: This contemporary B & B is in a wooded area with a view of Lake Taneycomo. Each of the four rooms offers king- or queen-sized beds and private baths. Two have private entrances. A separate mirrored spa room has soft lighting for romantic moods. And a game room offers a pinball machine and exercise treadmill. Breakfasts includes assorted homemade breads. Two people, $70. Open all year. Off Fall Creek Road, close to Missouri 76 and the Grand Palace. Hosts: Dick and Gigi House. HCR 5, Box 2368-2, Branson, MO 65616. Phone: 417-334-6873.

Cameron's Crag: Perched on a bluff overlooking Lake Taneycomo, this contemporary B & B offers three guest rooms, each with private entrances and baths. There are private spas available inside or on a deck overlooking the lake. Rates are $55 to $85 for two. Close to College of the Ozarks, three miles south of Branson off U.S. 65. Hosts: Kay and Glen Cameron. P.O. Box 526, Point Lookout, MO 65726. Phone: 417-335-8134; 800-933-8529.

Country Gardens: Across Lake Taneycomo from downtown Branson, you might see a great blue heron along the shore here. Breakfast on home-made granola or biscuits, waffles or crepes—or stay snuggled in one of the four-poster beds. Choose from the Rose Suite, with a private spa and two queen-sized beds; the Dogwood Suite, with a complete kitchen; or the Bittersweet Room, from which you can lounge in a spa on the deck. Each has a private entrance. There's a swimming pool and boat dock too. Rates for two, $75 to $95. Closed December 20 through February 20. Hosts: Pat and Bob Cameron. HCR 4, Box 2202, Branson, MO 65616. Phone: 417-334-8564; 800-727-0723.

Resorts & Condos

There are plenty of family-operated resorts in the area on Lake Taneycomo and Table Rock Lake for visitors interested in water sports. Nearby (15 miles west) Kimberling City also has many lake resorts. Note:

★ These are open year-round unless other-
  wise noted.
★ Advance reservations are a must from
  April through September.
★ While most have ground-level facilities

and doors wide enough to accommodate wheelchairs, many do not have bathroom railings.

I've picked a few that are most conveniently located close in, for hitting the country music show circuit. With one exception:

DON'T MISS!! *Big Cedar Lodge* is worth the drive 14 miles south of Branson just to look around and have a Bloody Mary by the pool. The resort, off U.S. 65 on Missouri 86, is also an exceptional place to stay. Its luxurious accommodations have the feel of an old-time hunting lodge. The spectacular complex of 133 rooms, cabins, and a lodge resides on 250 acres adjoining Table Rock Lake. Devil's Pool Restaurant, a marina, outdoor pools, riding stables, and nature trails, make this resort, owned by Bass Pro Shops of Springfield, Missouri, a special place. Lots of visiting stars stay here, including Waylon Jennings and Garth Brooks. Rates for two people range from $57 for a standard room to $750 a night for the 2500-square-foot Governor's Suite. Address: 612 Devil's Pool Road, Ridgedale, MO 65739. Phone: 417-335-2777.

Del Mar Resort: Across Lake Taneycomo from downtown Branson, these 14 cabins offer a quiet retreat where you can fish from the dock, rent a

boat, or lounge by the pool. The cabins with
kitchenettes range from $47 to $57 for two people. Closed the last two weeks of December. On
Lakeshore Drive next to Belle Rive, the palatial
home of popular romance novelist Janet Dailey.
HCR 4, Box 2193, Branson, MO 65616. Phone:
417-334-6241.

Fall Creek Resort: These 250 condos on Lake
Taneycomo are close to Buck Trent's Theater,
where you can catch breakfast and a 9 A.M. show.
The resort offers indoor and outdoor pools, tennis and volleyball courts, a private fishing dock
with rental boats. The condos are fully
equipped, including washer and dryer. But
they're not handicapped-equipped. One bedroom luxury condo, $74. Studio condo (like a
motel room with kitchenette) $58. Prices $10
lower in January and February. Three miles
south of Missouri 76 on Missouri 165, close to
Pointe Royale. Address: One Fall Creek Drive,
Branson, MO 65616. Phone: 417-334-6404; 800-
562-6636.

Lazy Valley Resort: Off Fall Creek Road, two
miles south of Missouri 76, with easy access to
theaters, these 16 one- and two-bedroom house-
keeping cabins offer a swimming pool, basket-
ball court, picnic tables and grills, and a private
dock with rental boats on Lake Taneycomo. Not
handicapped-equipped. Rates range from $42 to

$100 depending on the sleeping capacity of the cabin. HCR 5, Box 2168, Branson, MO 65616. Phone: 417-334-2397.

Lilley's Landing Resort: Twenty-two lakeside one- to four-bedroom kitchenette units on Lake Taneycomo, with convenient access from Fall Creek Road to the strip. In a beautiful setting across from tall bluffs, enjoy the pool, playground, and dock where you can fish or rent boats. Two people, $42, lakefront cabin $50. HCR 5, Box 2170, Branson, MO 65616. Phone: 334-6380; 800-284-2196.

Pointe Royale Condos: A private, gated resort and golf course where many of Branson's stars live. Visiting stars often stay in the condos. Five motel rooms and several one- and two-bedroom condos are available for nightly rentals. Two-bedroom condos for four people range from $90 to $152. One-bedrooms for two people range from $55 to $78. The motel ranges from $40 to $55 for two people. The condos have fully-equipped kitchens and are nicely furnished. Condo guests may take advantage of the pool, clubhouse, and lighted tennis courts. There also is a discount for guests on green fees for golf. Pointe Royale is on Missouri 165, three miles south of Missouri 76. Address: 4 Pointe Royale Drive, Branson, MO 65616. Phone: 417-334-5614. 800-962-4710.

Sammy Lane Resort: Since 1924, visitors interested in enjoying Lake Taneycomo have stayed
in these log cabins on the downtown lakefront.
Thirty-three modernized units with kitchens,
and six rooms in the lodge, are available. The
shady resort features a large (150-by-60-foot)
outdoor pool, hot tub, and fishing pier. A short
walk to restaurants, shopping, and marinas. Not
handicapped-equipped. Closed mid-December
until March 1. Two people, $40 to $60. Address:
320 E. Main Street, Branson, MO 65616. Phone:
417-334-3253.

Campgrounds

Many visitors to Branson arrive in motor
homes, and there are more than 6000 campsites
to accommodate them. I've listed the campsites
most easily accessible to Country Music Boulevard. Note:

★ Early reservations are essential.
★ Prices quoted are for full-hook-up sites.
  Tent sites also are available.
★ Open year-round unless otherwise
  noted.

Branson City Campground: This downtown campground on the Lake Taneycomo shore offers 350

sites with a playground and showers, picnic tables and grills. Close to the city park's swimming pool and tennis courts. Full-service site, $13. City Hall, Branson, MO 65616. Phone: 417-334-2915; 334-8857.

Branson KOA Musicland Kampground: Close to Country Music Boulevard shows, this 109-site campground offers a pool and playground, laundry and showers. On Gretna Road, just north of Missouri 76. Open April 1 through November 1. Full-service sites, $21.95. Gretna Road, Branson, MO 65616. Phone: 417-334-0848.

Compton's Ridge Campground: This 223-site campground on Missouri 265 is conveniently close to Silver Dollar City. Three pools and a wading pool, playground, tennis court, recreation hall, laundry, showers, a convenience store, a water slide, and Sunday church services make this place special. Also offers free shuttle service to Silver Dollar City. Closed November through March. Full-service site, $17.50 to 19.50. HCR 9, Box 1180, Branson, MO 65616. Phone: 417-338-2911; 800-233-8648.

Cooper Creek Resort and Campground: On Lake Taneycomo off Fall Creek Road, two miles south of Missouri 76. Convenient access to shows. Two swimming pools, laundry and shower facilities, grocery store, fishing docks with boat rental, and a playground. Full-service site, 1992 rates, $15.75. HCR 5, Box 2204 B, Branson, MO 65616. Phone: 417-334-4871.

Old Shepherd's Campground: On Missouri 76 west of the strip toward Silver Dollar City. This shady campground has a pool, game room, playground, and a trail leading to Shepherd of the Hills Homestead next door. Also features a convenience store, laundry, and showers. Church service is offered as well. Full service, 1992 rate, $16.00. P.O. Box 97, Branson, MO 65616. Phone: 417-334-7692.

Ozark Country Campground: On Missouri 165, three miles south of Missouri 76, you'll find an Olympic-size pool, a large pavilion with grill, playground, laundry and showers, and free morning coffee. Near Pzazz Restaurant at Pointe Royale. Full-service site, $17. HCR 5, Box 1709, Branson, MO 65616. Phone: 417-334-4681.

Presley's Campground: Next door to Presley's Mountain Music Jubilee and Presley's Cafeteria, this campground offers a pool and playground, laundry and showers. Full-service site, $16. Address: 2920 Highway 76 West, Branson, MO 65616. Phone: 417-334-3447.

Silver Dollar City Campground: On Missouri 265 near Silver Dollar City, this 185-site park offers a convenience store, pool, playground, 600-foot

water slide, game room, and showers. Free shuttles to Silver Dollar City. Closed mid-December
to April 1. Full-service site, $18.50. Highway
265, Branson, MO 65616. Phone: 417-338-8189;
800-477-5164.

Houseboats

For a real getaway experience, stay on a
houseboat while you visit Branson. Several marinas on Table Rock Lake rent luxurious fifty-foot
houseboats by the day or week. The houseboats
are floating hotels, furnished with kitchens,
dishes, linens, grills, and safety equipment. The
boats can sleep up to ten adults. Most feature
fully-equipped kitchens with microwaves, stereo
systems, and ship-to-shore radios. They're also
air-conditioned and have upper decks for sun-
ning and diving. Some even have water slides.

Don't worry if you're not an experienced
boater. The marina crew gives first-timers in-
structions and a short "check-out cruise." The
boats are easy to maneuver, and Table Rock
Lake is generally calm water. If you can drive a
car, you can get around in one of these.

With 750 miles of shoreline, there are plenty
of places to explore, secluded coves where you
can fish or swim, and marinas about every ten

miles for supplies, groceries, and gas. All of this within a twenty-mile radius of the music shows.

Prices for rentals depend on the length of the rental and the time of year, but range from about $110 to $350 a day.

TIP! Pets are not allowed on houseboats.

Houseboat Holidays: Located at the Baxter Recreation Area, about 18 miles southwest of Branson on "H" Highway near Lampe, Missouri. Open March 1 through November 1. Rates range from $395 for a two-day rental between March 16–May 14 and September 14–November 2, to $1695 for a week during peak season, June 12–August 16. HCR 1, Box 205, Lampe, MO 65681. Phone: 800-833-5214.

Table Rock Lake Houseboat Vacation Rental: Here you can rent 64-foot houseboats that sleep up to ten. They feature 1½ bathrooms, complete with a shower and bath, of course. The boats store 400 gallons of water. They have gas grills, microwave, fully-equipped kitchens, stereo and television. Rates range from $500 for two nights from September 15 through May 15, up to $1100 for three nights during peak season from May 15 through September 15. They also rent 32-foot cruisers for overnight trips—4 P.M. departure to 11 A.M. return time. They range from about $110 a day from September through May to $220 a day from May through September. Located at

Gage's Long Creek Marina, 10 miles south of Branson on Lake Road 86-26. P.O. Box 6545, Branson, MO 65616. Phone: 417-335-3042; 800-622-3246.

IMPORTANT ADDRESSES & PHONE NUMBERS

Branson/Lakes Area Chamber of
   Commerce
P.O. Box 220
Branson, MO 65616
Phone: 417-334-4136

To order visitors information: 1-900-334-884-2726. Each call costs $1.50 per minute. Average call is three minutes.

To call Lodging Locator for computer lodging information: 417-336-4466.

The Visitors Center is located on the north side of Branson. From U.S. 65, exit at Missouri 248. A large sign marks the center, just west of the exit.

Also:

* ★ Branson Police Department: 417-334-3300
* ★ Taney County Sheriff's Department: 417-546-2191

★ National Weather Service, Springfield, MO: 417-869-4491

HISTORY

The story of Branson's development is entertainment in its own right. Who would have thought a book called *Shepherd of the Hills* and a cave tour attraction would grow into a town that attracts more visitors each year than the Grand Canyon?

A lot of residents of Branson didn't foresee this kind of growth. Instead, the growth of Branson as a tourist destination was forged by the natural beauty of the countryside, some fortuitous circumstances, and the work of several families who built their businesses from meager beginnings.

In 1803, when the Ozarks became part of the United States, Osage Indians peopled the White River basin. In 1882, Reuben Branson, a schoolteacher from eastern Missouri, opened a store and established the post office. For many years, logging was the primary industry in the area. Branson's riverfront was the production site for wagons, boxes, spokes, railroad ties, and veneer.

With the coming of the Missouri Pacific Railroad in 1903, the area's scenic bluffs, streams, and valleys became more accessible to vacationers. When Branson was incorporated in 1912, the population was 1200 residents. Now, eighty years later, the population of 3700 play host to more than 5 million visitors each year.

The growth of the tourism industry in Branson may be marked from the 1907 publishing of Harold Bell Wright's *The Shepherd of the Hills*. Readers of the book came to learn more about the lifestyle depicted in his novel, set in the Mutton Hollow area in Roark Valley. Visitors came by train to Hollister, to the train station now preserved as City Hall. They stayed in tourist camps because hotel accommodations were limited in the early years.

By 1913, the Powersite Dam had turned a section of the White River into Lake Taneycomo, so Branson, Hollister, and Rockaway Beach became a popular lakeshore destination.

In the late fifties another dam was built, forming Table Rock Lake above Lake Taneycomo. To the joy of fishing enthusiasts, the flow of water from the bottom of Table Rock turned Taneycomo into a cold-water lake, providing an ideal climate for trout, while bass, crappie, and other fish could be found in next-door Table Rock.

In 1960 three families opened businesses that would become the core of entertainment. Hugo and Mary Herschend bought the long-popular

Marvel Cave, ten miles west of Branson, and opened an old-time Ozarks' village featuring an 1890s steam train above the cave. They called the place Silver Dollar City. Today it has grown into a 90-acre entertainment complex that attracts millions of visitors a year.

A few miles east of Silver Dollar City, Bruce and Mary Trimble opened an outdoor pageant based on Wright's book. Today, Shepherd of the Hills Homestead and Outdoor Theater is a mainstay of Branson. Also in 1960, the five Mabe brothers began performing a country music show called "The Baldknobbers" in a 50-seat auditorium in Branson's City Hall.

Eight years later, in 1968, they followed the Presley's Mountain Music Jubilee in opening a theater on Missouri 76. Both shows are still family-owned, with several generations on stage every night. Both theaters have grown to seat nearly 2000 people and are sold out most nights of the season.

Branson was on an irreversible course that would slowly snowball until the 1991 explosion. The 1970s saw the addition of three theaters. In 1981 three more theaters were built, which now house Boxcar Willie, Mickey Gilley, and Cristy Lane. In 1983, Swiss Villa amphitheater opened 15 miles south of Branson in Lampe. The theater seated 7500, and over the next few years many country stars appeared there, including

Willie Nelson, George Strait, Reba McEntire, and Tanya Tucker.

That same year, Branson got its first nationally-known star on Missouri 76 when Roy Clark opened his Celebrity Theatre. Clark, the longtime host of television's "Hee Haw," appeared 100 dates a year himself and brought in others, like Conway Twitty, Roger Miller—and some who now are permanent residents of Branson, like Mel Tillis and Ray Stevens.

Between 1983 and 1991 ten more theaters opened on Country Music Boulevard, and Branson's entertainers gained national recognition. The Lowe Sisters and Boxcar Willie made appearances on Nashville's Grand Ole Opry. In 1987, Branson shows were featured on "Nashville Now" and ABC's "Good Morning America."

Then came 1991, the year the city of Branson issued building permits for $84 million in new construction. The previous record was $14.5 million in 1988.

Silver Dollar City started construction on the 4000-seat Grand Palace. Ray Stevens, Moe Bandy, Buck Trent, and Jim Stafford opened their own theaters. Mel Tillis built his new 2100-seat glitter dome. And noncountry crooner Andy Williams broke ground for his 2000-seat Moon River Theatre.

Williams's immediate success brought other

pop artists to town. In 1992, Wayne Newton announced he would spend part of the year in a theater he would build. Television and musical star John Davidson performed matinees at the Jim Stafford Theatre and may soon have his own theater. Bobby Vinton is building the Blue Velvet Theatre. And crooner Tony Orlando is tying yellow ribbons to Branson's oak trees around a 2000-seat theater planned for 1993.

As the growth continues, rumors are rampant about which entertainer will arrive next.

As the theaters, restaurants, and motels have sprung up, city and county planners scramble to keep up with environmental concerns to protect the beauty and serenity of the Ozarks, to make sure the lakes' water remains an inviting place on a hot July day.

Traffic on the five miles of the two-lane Missouri 76 strip grew to near-gridlock proportions. Now the county and city are working to widen side roads and add connecting routes to provide an alternative for the people who don't want to travel slowly along the strip to view the many attractions there.

The state highway department took a look at Branson's contribution to state sales tax revenue and jumped into the roadwork with plans to widen U.S. 65 from Springfield to Branson to four lanes, and to build a four-lane loop around the strip that will give drivers more options.

These days, when people gather in Branson, be they visitors or hometown folks, the town's growth is often a subject for speculation. Some have visions of another Los Angeles sprouting up around a little Hollywood. Others think the growth will soon level off.

But many of the performers who are here, and those who are considering locating here, reflect what Mel Tillis has to say: "This is the place to be. What else could I want? I have lots of loyal fans who want to come here to see me; I can make a lot more money without the overhead of managers and agents; I can go home to my family and sleep in my own bed every night; and weekends, I go f-f-fishin'."

☆ **NASHVILLE** ☆

Here's a word-association quiz. Try it on your friends: Say "Nashville." The most common response? "Country Music."

"Music City USA" has earned it title. The down-home, grassroots music reflecting the cares and concerns of middle America became a genre recognized nationwide with the advent of radio. And Nashville's place in country music began in 1925, when radio station WSM-AM 650 began broadcasting a Saturday night hoedown. That first broadcast featured Uncle Jimmy Thompson, a Tennessee fiddler.

In 1927 announcer George Hay dubbed the program "The Grand Ole Opry," and the program has aired every Saturday night without exception since that time.

Around that basis grew an industry. Now more

than 200 recording and production businesses call Nashville home—as do many of country music's performers.

The Grand Ole Opry, now in new quarters at the Opryland USA complex, still does live shows every Friday and Saturday. And there are lots of other activities for country music fans in Nashville.

★ Wander through the halls of the *Country Music Hall of Fame and Museum* to see the gold records and other memorabilia of country's best-known stars.

★ DON'T MISS!! the now vacant *Ryman Auditorium,* home of the Opry from 1943 to 1974.

★ Visit the Opryland USA theme park, where you can attend a live telecast of "Nashville Now."

★ Spend some time in one of a dozen museums of entertainer memorabilia, including the *House of Cash,* where you can see Johnny's "One Piece at a Time" Cadillac, built from parts dating from 1949 to 1973 on a 1968 chassis.

★ DON'T MISS!! spending some time in the historic downtown district. A visit to Nashville can't be complete without spending an hour at *Tootsie's Orchid Lounge.* Close to the Ryman Auditorium,

this old bar has played host to all the
country music greats.

★ There's plenty of country music nightlife,
from Boots Randolph's lounge to the Ernest Tubb Record Shop Midnight Jamboree.

Plus—Nashville's a big city with fascinating
nooks and crannies for the curious visitor to explore. Nashville residents are proud of the diversity that may see a rap group performing two
blocks from an Emmylou Harris concert, while
just down the street visitors may be attending a
performance of the Nashville Ballet, the Nashville Opera Company, or the Nashville Symphony. Where else could you find country guitar
legend Chet Atkins collaborating with a professional modern dance troupe?

GETTING THERE

In the heart of Tennessee, Nashville is within a
600-mile radius of half the population of the
United States. Interstates 40, 24, and 65 con-
verge in Nashville.

Nashville International Airport, eight miles
southeast of downtown, served 7.4 million passengers in 1990. It's an American Airlines hub,
served by eleven other major airlines, including

American Eagle, United, Delta, and USAir Express.

Nashville is served by Greyhound Bus Lines. Amtrak trains do not offer passenger service to Nashville.

GETTING AROUND

The Metropolitan Transit Authority operates bus service throughout the city. It also operates the Nashville Trolley Company, with service from Riverfront Park downtown to Music Row. Fare is 50 to 75 cents. For a route and schedule information, call 615-242-4433.

There are 13 car rental agencies, including Alamo, Avis, Budget, and Hertz at the International Airport.

There also are a dozen taxicab companies, but the country music venues are scattered within a twelve-mile radius, making constant taxi travel a budget-breaker. Taxi fare from the airport to downtown is $13 to $17.

Country music attractions are located primarily in three sections of town: the downtown historic district, the Music Row area two miles southwest of downtown, and the Opryland area, nine miles northeast of downtown. Access between the downtown and Music Row areas and the Opryland area is easy by taking Interstate 65 north to the Briley Parkway. The parkway is a four-lane divided road. Exit ramps to Opryland are clearly marked.

Visitors also will want to take Interstate 65 north to the Hendersonville area twenty miles north of downtown Nashville. This is where you'll find Conway Twitty's "Twitty City," Johnny Cash's museum, and Music Village, a 1700-seat live-performance theater. Exits to those attractions, via the Vietnam Veterans Memorial Parkway, are marked by road signs.

TIP! For driving with the greatest ease, pick a motel in the Opryland area. Some of the one-way downtown streets can get confusing if you're trying to find your hotel at night after a show.

Several tour bus companies offer package tours of sites in Nashville. Tour possibilities include the Ryman Auditorium, Music Row, the Grand Ole Opry, Opryland, drive-bys of homes of the stars, the Hermitage, the historic downtown district, the Governor's Mansion, and Fort Nashborough. The tour packages range from three hours to a full day. Prices range from $7.50 to $28 per person. Most are able to accommodate the disabled:

Country & Western/Gray Lines Tours: 2416 Music Valley Drive. Phone: 615-256-1200; 800-251-1864.

Grand Ole Opry Tours: 2810 Opryland Drive. Phone: 615-889-9490.

Johnny Walker Tours: 97 Wallace Road. Phone: 615-834-8585; 800-722-1524.

Weather: Summertime in Nashville can be warm and humid. Average daytime high temperature is 89 degrees. Nighttime lows average 69 degrees. Average summer humidity is 58 percent. Spring and fall are the most moderate times for visiting Nashville.

Winter temperatures can be chilly, with a daytime average high of 46 degrees and a low of 27. But lots of sunny days beat the average too. If snowfall occurs, it's usually in January or February, and usually isn't heavy.

Dress: Casual dress is the norm for tourist attractions, but since it's a fairly cosmopolitan city, it's a good idea for men to bring a jacket and tie in case dinner at an upscale restaurant sounds appealing. A sweater for evenings, even in the summer, is a good idea.

HOW TO STRETCH $100

(Prices are for one person and include taxes
and tips.)

Fiddlers Inn North, single room	$37.39
Breakfast, Country Star Cafe (two eggs, bacon, toast and coffee)	2.07
Ryman Auditorium Tour	2.50
Country Music Hall of Fame and Museum	7.50
Souvenir—A Conway Twitty thimble	3.86
Lunch, Windows on the Cumberland (an avocado sandwich with sprouts!!)	5.88
Elvis Presley Museum	4.00
Hank Williams, Jr. Museum	4.00
A cold beer at Tootsie's Orchid Lounge	1.75
Nashville Toy Museum	3.50
Dinner and show at Boots Randolph's	26.34
	$98.79

POSSIBLE SPLURGE!! A visit to Tower Records, a huge store that carries every record, tape, or disk I've ever hunted for. At least $50!

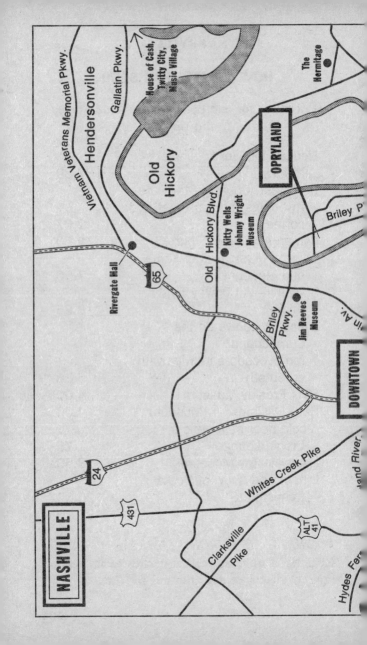

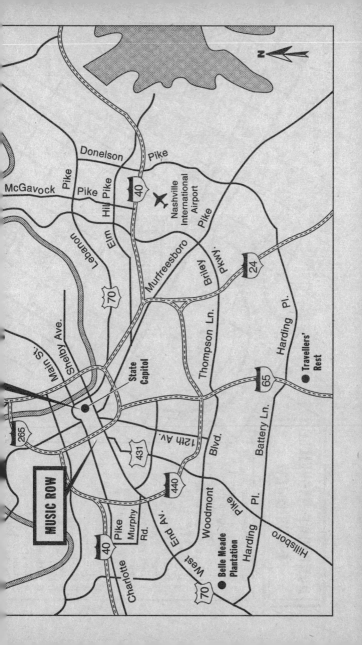

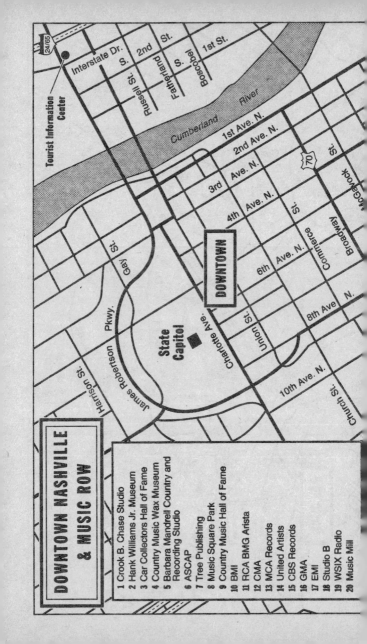

DOWNTOWN NASHVILLE & MUSIC ROW

1 Crook B. Chase Studio
2 Hank Williams Jr. Museum
3 Car Collectors Hall of Fame
4 Country Music Wax Museum
5 Barbara Mandrell Country and Recording Studio
6 ASCAP
7 Tree Publishing
8 Music Square Park
9 Country Music Hall of Fame
10 BMI
11 RCA BMG Arista
12 CMA
13 MCA Records
14 United Artists
15 CBS Records
16 GMA
17 EMI
18 Studio B
19 WSIX Radio
20 Music Mill

Tourist Information Center

Interstate Dr.

Russell St.

2nd St.

Fatherland St.

Boscobel St.

1st St.

Cumberland River

1st Ave. N.

2nd Ave. N.

3rd Ave. N.

4th Ave. N.

6th Ave. N.

8th Ave. N.

10th Ave. N.

70

McGavock St.

Commerce St.

Broadway

Union St.

Church St.

Charlotte Ave.

DOWNTOWN

State Capitol

James Robertson Pkwy.

Gay St.

Harrison St.

24/65

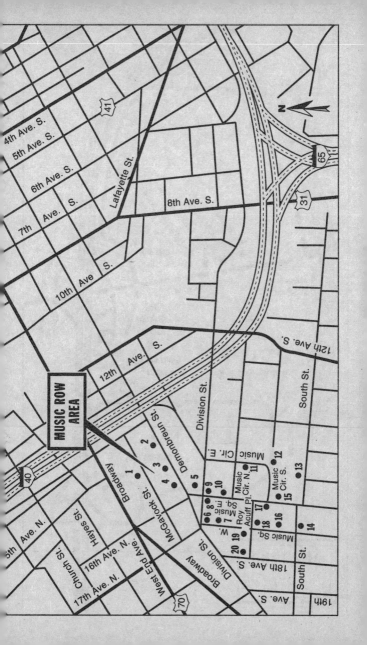

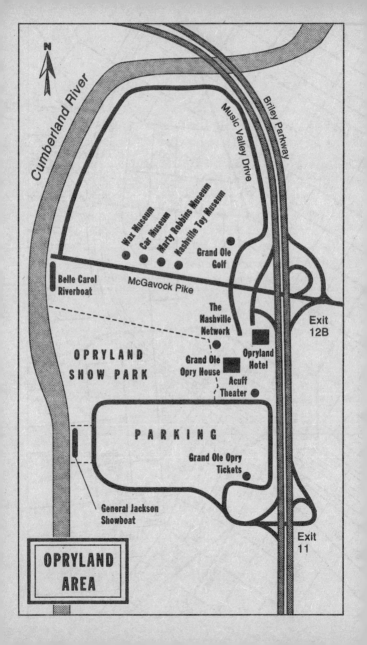

OPRYLAND USA

Opryland USA is the 757-acre home to a theme park called Opryland, the Grand Ole Opry, a live country music radio show, the Nashville Network, the opulent Opryland Hotel, WSM-AM and FM radio, Country Music Television, and the General Jackson showboat.

It all originated with radio station WSM-650 AM. When the station went on the air in 1925, the call letters stood for "We Shield Millions," the theme of the station's original owner, National Life and Accident Insurance. Within two months the station originated a show that became the Grand Ole Opry, a country music show that's still on the air every Friday and Saturday nights, live from Opryland USA.

It's the longest-running regularly scheduled radio show ever. On Saturday nights viewers of the Nashville Network Opry Live telecast see a half-hour segment of the show. The Grand Ole Opry moved to its present quarters at Opryland USA in 1974.

The 120-acre theme park draws about two million guests a year to stage productions, rides, shops, and restaurants. Also on the grounds, the 1891-room Opryland Hotel—an attraction in its own right, the Nashville Network and Country Music Television stations, the 1000-passenger General Jackson paddle-wheel showboat, and museums: the Roy Acuff Museum, Minnie Pearl Museum, and Grand Ole Opry Museum. There are lots of special events at Opryland too, including the concert series at the 3500-seat Chevrolet/ Geo Celebrity Theater in Opryland. Visitors should plan a couple of days at the park to catch all the music shows and see the sights.

The Grand Ole Opry

DON'T MISS!! The longest-running radio show is still on the airwaves, and the live broadcasts attracted more than 800,000 people to the audience last year. The "new" Grand Ole Opry House, built inside Opryland USA in 1974, cost $13.5 million. Every Friday and Saturday, stars from its roster of 60 members perform in two shows. On Saturday nights a half-hour segment is broadcast live on the Nashville Network. There also are matinees part of the year from 3 to 5 P.M. on Tuesdays, Thursdays, Saturdays, and Sundays.

Visitors are reminded that this is a radio show. The stage is undecorated, "costumes" are whatever the entertainer feels like wearing. And at one side of the stage is the announcer, who reads commercials on-air between the performances.

The audience is invited to walk up to the stage to take still photos of the performers, but camcorders are not allowed.

There are two shows Saturday nights year-round. The first evening show runs from 6:30 to 9 P.M. The second show (separate admission) goes from 9:30 P.M. to midnight. Friday performances: January 3–April 24 and November 6–December 25, one show, 7:30 to 11 P.M. May 1–October 30, two shows, 6:30 to 9 P.M. and 9:30 P.M. to midnight.

Matinees: Two-hour matinees feature eight or nine artists in a concert-style performance. Matinees are not broadcast.

★ Saturday matinees: April 11–July 25 and September 5–October 31, one show, 3 to 5 P.M.
★ Sunday matinees: June 14–August 9, one show, 3 to 5 P.M.
★ Tuesday matinees: May 26–September 1, one show, 3 to 5 P.M.
★ Thursday matinees: May 28–September 3, one show, 3 to 5 P.M.

Admission
BUDGET ALERT!! For a chance to see a few superstars of country music live along with the nostalgia of this long-lived radio show, this is a bargain.

* Main floor/first balcony: $15 evenings, $13 matinees
* Upper balcony: $13 evenings, $11 matinees
* Children under 4 admitted free

TIP!! Reserve tickets to the Opry as soon as you know trip dates. They often sell out, especially during the summer. Seats are assigned according to earliest purchase date.

Each show features about twenty artists singing one to three numbers. Artist lineup is scheduled the week before the show. Surprises are part of the fun at the Opry. You never know who may drop by.

To order tickets, contact Grand Ole Opry Ticket Office, 2808 Opryland Drive, Nashville, TN 37214. Phone: 615-889-3060.

Music Shows

Here's a rundown on the other music shows available in the park. All performances are included in the price of admission EXCEPT the Country Concert Series presented in the Chevrolet/Geo Celebrity Theater.

* "Country Music U.S.A." In the Theater by the Lake, this 45-minute show pays

tribute to stars by impersonating such greats as Patsy Cline, Hank Williams Sr., Garth Brooks, Reba McEntire, and more. A cast of 16.

★ "For Me and My Gal" In the 1500-seat Acuff Theater, a cast of 20 and orchestra of 16 features music from the gay nineties to World War I in this 45-minute show.

★ "Way Out West" This show in the Durango Theater features a cast of 18 in a 45-minute production of western characters and songs from Broadway, TV, and movies.

★ "And The Winner Is . . ." In the American Music Theater, features songs that have been award winners in movies, TV, recordings, and on Broadway. Performed by a cast of 18.

★ "Rockin' U.S.A." In the Chevrolet/Geo Celebrity Theater, this 45-minute show highlights rock 'n' roll classics from Buddy Holly, Elvis, and more.

★ "Sing the Glory Down" At the New Orleans Bandstand, this 25-minute show features gospel music from traditional to contemporary.

★ "The Mike Snider Show" Also at the New Orleans Bandstand, "Hee Haw" regular Mike Snider provides 25 minutes of banjo pickin' and country humor.

★ "The Country and Bluegrass Show" At the Country and Bluegrass Theater, this 25-minute show features mountain folk tunes, country songs, and humor.

★ "Kickin' Country" In the Durango Theater, listen to a six-piece band do contemporary country with a Cajun flavor. Trick fiddling too.

★ Opryland's Country Concert Series: The 3500-seat Chevrolet/Geo Celebrity Theater has a lineup of big-name entertainers throughout the summer. Among the entertainers scheduled in 1993 are Lee Greenwood (June 6), Conway Twitty (July 24–25), Gary Morris (August 23–25), Diamond Rio (September 4–5) and Lorrie Morgan (October 23–24). On June 21–25, the television program "Nashville Now" will be broadcast live from the concert stage. All seats are reserved, and the concerts cost an extra $5.50 to ticketed park attendees. You must pay park admission to attend.

Other acts slated to perform include:
Spring weekends: Patty Loveless, Emmylou Harris, Hal Ketchum, Doug Stone, Crystal

Gayle, Marie Osmond, Holly Dunn, Jerry Clower and Joe Diffie.

Summer days: Holly Dunn, Tracy Lawrence, Lee Greenwood, Collin Raye, Louise Mandrell, Ricky Skaggs, Paul Overstreet, Lorrie Morgan, Sammy Kershaw, Joe Diffie, Tanya Tucker, Sweethearts of the Rodeo, Hal Ketchum, Mark Chesnutt, Marie Osmond, Crystal Gayle, Jerry Clower, Conway Twitty, Patty Loveless, Marty Stuart, Doug Stone, Gary Morris, and Lee Roy Parnell.

Autumn weekends include Diamond Rio, Joe Diffie, Forester Sisters, Doug Stone, Conway Twitty, Crystal Gayle, Marie Osmond, Emmylou Harris, Lee Greenwood, Lorrie Morgan, and Louise Mandrell.

For exact schedules and reservations, write Opryland USA Customer Service, 2802 Opryland Drive, Nashville, TN 37214. Phone: 615-889-6611.

The Opryland Hotel

DON'T MISS!! This 1891-room $140-million hotel is a must to visit and stroll through, even if it's out of the budget price range for lodging.

The hotel covers more than thirty acres and has 320,000 square feet of meeting and exhibit space. The hotel has fourteen restaurants and lounges, three swimming pools, and sixteen incredible gift shops. If that's not enough, there's the 18-hole championship golf course.

DON'T MISS!! *The Victorian Conservatory*, crowned by a one-acre skylight, is a garden under glass that covers nearly two acres. Follow the pathways past waterfalls and rocky coves beside the flowing stream. Pick a bench for some quiet meditation or a romantic chat.

The architects who designed the garden visited conservatories in England, Scotland, Italy, and Canada to study the traditional gathering place for the poshest nineteenth-century soirees. The garden is filled by thousands of tropical plants, more than 200 species. There are fifteen types of palm trees, four kinds of banana trees— even a sprinkling of orange trees. The temperature is controlled at 71 degrees, so it's a wonderful respite from outside temperatures both summer and winter.

DON'T MISS!! The other spectacular area of the hotel, between the Conservatory and the lobby, is the *Cascades Water Garden*. Also, crowned by a huge skylight, this two-acre space houses three waterfalls, ranging from 23 to 35 feet high, and the Dancing Waters fountains. On the elevated Promenade, visitors can walk through the forty-foot-high mountain down to the restaurant and revolving lounge. Have a cocktail in the lounge while you watch the fountains' changing patterns. In the evenings the fountains are synchronized with performances of harpists. More than 449 species of tropical plants make visitors feel they are truly in an exotic locale.

Opryland Restaurants

Cascades Restaurant in the Cascades Water Garden is open daily from 6:30 A.M. for breakfast, lunch, and dinner.

Old Hickory: An elegant dining room where a jacket and tie is "preferred." Located near the lobby, reservations are recommended.

Rachel's Kitchen: Family dining, open at 6:30 A.M. for breakfast, lunch, and dinner near the lobby.

Rhett's Restaurant: Traditional southern menu, open at 6:30 A.M. for breakfast, lunch, or dinner in the Conservatory.

TIP!: All of these restaurants tend to be a bit pricey (lunch choices ranging from $5 to $12). If you're on a tight budget, have lunch instead of dinner in this wonderful atmosphere.

Opryland Lounges

Jack Daniel's Saloon: In the Conservatory. Open Monday through Saturday, 11 A.M. to 2 A.M.; Sundays, noon to 1 A.M. This is a fun place for a late-night beverage.

Pickin' Parlor: Open Mondays through Saturdays, 11 A.M. to 1 A.M.; Sundays, 4 P.M. to 1 A.M., with live country entertainment.

Stage Door Lounge: Near the main lobby, this lounge features a variety of live music performers. Open Mondays through Saturdays 11 A.M. to 2 A.M.; Sundays, noon to 2 A.M.

Opryland Shops

Aunt Pitty Pats: A great assortment of classy dolls and seemingly every figurine ever made. At the entrance to the Conservatory. Open daily 7:30 A.M. to 9 P.M.

Chantilly's Lace: Fine, really "fine," lingerie. Open daily 8 A.M. to 9 P.M. In the Cascades lower area.

Crown Clock: A grandfather clock may be too big to take home in the trunk, but Crown Clock will ship. Open Mondays through Fridays, 9 A.M. to 9 P.M.; Saturdays and Sundays, 9 A.M. to 5 P.M. At the entrance to the Conservatory.

Genuine Jack Daniel's Goods: All kinds of souvenirs with the Jack Daniel's logo. Open daily 8 A.M. to 9 P.M. in the lobby area.

Springhouse Golf Shop: At the entrance to the Conservatory. Everything for the golfing enthusiast. Open daily 8 A.M. to 9 P.M.

If You Decide to Stay . . .

Rates for two people range from $159 to $189. Address: 2800 Opryland Drive, Nashville, TN 37214. Phone: 615-889-1000.

Museums at Opryland USA

Admission to these museums is free for visitors to Opryland.

Roy Acuff Musical Collection and Museum: Roy Acuff, "King of Country Music," joined the Grand Ole Opry in 1938. In 1942, Acuff and songwriter Fred Rose, composer of hits like "Blue Eyes Crying in the Rain" and "Take These Chains from My Heart," started Nashville's first music publishing company. Acuff became one of the most popular Opry performers and performed many of his own songs, like "Wabash Cannonball," "Great Speckled Bird," and "A Vagabond's Dream." In 1985, Acuff sold the publishing company to Opryland USA, Inc. Acuff died in 1992.

His museum boasts more than 275 stringed

instruments, including an 1880s Martin guitar. There are family heirlooms, a collection of Acuff's yo-yos, and lots of other memorabilia from his long career. The museum opened in 1978.

The Minnie Pearl Museum: The "Queen of Country Comedy" is the focus of this museum, which is next to Acuff's. The exhibits chronicle Minnie's development from the real-life Sarah Cannon in Centerville, Tennessee, through her start on the Grand Ole Opry stage in 1940. The museum moved to Opryland in 1989 from the former site on Music Row.

Grand Ole Opry Museum: Electronic displays highlight the rise to fame of this radio show. And it focuses on the many performers over the years who graced the stage of the Ryman Auditorium in downtown Nashville, including Patsy Cline, Marty Robbins, and Hank Snow. Porter Wagoner narrates a video history of the Opry. The museum opened in 1992.

General Jackson Showboat

DON'T MISS!! The 14-mile round-trip ride down the Cumberland River on this 300-foot, four-story showboat is a wonderful change of pace while in Nashville—and you still get country music.

On board this year-round attraction, you'll find strolling musicians, stage productions, and good food and drink. The morning and noon cruises offer an optional buffet. The evening cruise features a three-course dinner. The later Southern Nights Cruise offers an optional steak dinner. There are also snack bars on board where you can get a hot dog, potato chips, an apple dumpling, and a Coke for $5.50.

The original *General Jackson* was the first steamboat to make port in Nashville, arriving in 1819. It made regular runs from Nashville to New Orleans. Opryland's *General Jackson* arrived in 1985. It's twice as large as its namesake, measuring 300 feet in length and 63 feet in width. The working paddle wheel is twenty feet across and contains more than twenty tons of white pine.

While the restaurant show is a good one, if you want a change of pace, sip a cool brew on the front of the main deck, put your feet up on the railing and let one of the snappy deckhands like Howard Stenson Jr. point out the passing sights along the Cumberland. Watch for Demonbreun's Cave, where some of the first settlers in this area took refuge from Indians in the 1770s.

Morning (8 A.M.) and midday (11:30 A.M.) cruises: Each two-hour cruise features Shotgun Red, of Nashville Network fame, in a country comedy variety show with Shotgun's creator, Steve Hall. And, if you choose, you can enjoy this with an optional breakfast or lunch buffet.

Evening Cruise (7 P.M.): This three-hour cruise features a three-course prime rib dinner in the Victorian Theater with entertainment from the General Jackson Showstoppers, ranging from Broadway tunes to country to rock 'n' roll.

Southern Nights Cruise (10:30 P.M.): If you'd rather stroll the decks and enjoy the stars, this 1½-hour cruise is offered, but doesn't include the stage entertainment. There is a band on deck for dancing. An optional steak dinner is available.

Admission: Prices are for passengers over age three. Prices do not include tax (8 percent) and tips.

* ★ Early-morning and midday cruise is $14.95. The optional breakfast buffet is $7.75; optional lunch buffet, $8.50.
* ★ Evening cruise, which includes dinner, is $36.95; children ages 4 through 11, $28.95.

★ Southern Nights cruise is $14.95. Add $13.80 for optional steak dinner.

For reservations, call 615-889-6611.

Rides at the Opryland Theme Park

Among the highlights are:

★ Chaos. The park's newest ride, added in 1989, is an indoor roller coaster combined with audiovisual technology.
★ Grizzly River Rampage. Added in 1981, rafts take visitors down a raging whitewater river.
★ Old Mill Scream. A water ride that takes guests in 20-passenger boats to a splashdown from a sixty-foot-tall mountain.
★ Wabash Cannonball. A roller coaster featuring two 360-degree corkscrew loops. The ride reaches a top speed of 55 mph.
★ Flume Zoom. Get wet!
★ Opryland Sky Ride. A tame skylift that gives guests a bird's-eye view of the park.
★ Opryland Railroad. A pleasant open-air train ride through the park.
★ Tennessee Waltz Swing Ride. For those

who are comfortable going around in cir-
cles.
★ Several rides designed for youngsters including the low-speed drive-yourself Little Deuce Coupe track.

There are lots of activities designed for the
tykes too, including Professor U.B. Sharp, who
entertains with magic tricks from his Musical
Magical Marvel Mobile. Another magic show
takes place at the Laughin' Place Theater, and
there are puppet shows at the Carousel Theater.
And a petting zoo too.

Dining in Opryland

BUDGET ALERT!! There's plenty of food
available in the park, but with small Cokes going
for $1.15 and an ordinary hot dog for $2.75, it can
add up to feed a family. The best buy is Opry
Inn. It's southern-style cafeteria food—including
side dishes of fried green tomatoes. A typical
meal for an adult, with salad, vegetable, meat,
and dessert, runs about $7. They also serve
breakfast.

Shopping: There are places to buy souvenirs, but
shopping isn't the star of the show here. Plenty

of Shotgun Red dolls available. For a selection of interesting shops, try the Opryland Hotel.

Carnival Games: Opryland has all the old-time carnival games that county fairs offered, including shooting galleries, softball toss, ring toss—even a fellow who guesses your age and weight. Seems like nearly everyone wins a prize worth about the $2 it costs to have him guess.

Special Events, 1993

February 24–28: 12th Annual Heart of Country Antiques Show. The Ryman Exhibit Hall in the Opryland Hotel is the scene for more than 150 dealers of furniture, fine and folk art, textiles and eighteenth- and nineteenth-century Americana. Seminars and lectures on Wednesday and Thursday. Admission: $7. Advance tickets are recommended. Briley Parkway, Exit 12B. Contact Richard Kramer, Show Manager, 427 Midvale Avenue, St. Louis, MO 63130. Phone: 314-862-1091.

April 3–4 and 10–11: Easter at Opryland. Lots of activities for children, including an Easter egg hunt, egg decorating, and visits by the Easter Bunny. Contact Opryland Customer Service,

2802 Opryland Drive, Nashville, TN 37214.
Phone: 615-889-6700.

April 22–24: 17th Annual Opryland American
Music Festival at the Grand Ole Opry House in
Opryland USA features more than 100 high
school bands and choruses from across the country. Contact American Music Festival, Opryland,
2802 Opryland Drive, Nashville, TN 37214.
Phone: 615-889-6600.

May 29–30: Opryland Gospel Jubilee. More than
a dozen gospel groups mark the beginning of the
theme park's season. Opryland's gospel quartet,
the Cumberland Boys, host the event. Contact
Opryland Customer Service, 2802 Opryland
Drive, Nashville, TN 37214. Phone: 615-889-
6700.

June 18–20: 6th Annual Southern Heritage Antique Show and Sale. In Ryman Exhibit Hall B
at the Opryland Hotel, visitors will find 25,000
square feet of space filled with antiques from
dealers in more than twenty states. Everything
from toys and tools, to cut glass and country furniture. Admission $4; children under 12 free.
Contact Ellie Mead, 213 N. Main Street, Good-
lettsville, TN 37072. Phone: 615-859-5261.

July 2–5: Independence Celebration at Opryland. Fireworks, flags, and patriotic music. Contact Opryland Customer Service, 2802 Opryland

Drive, Nashville, TN 37214. Phone: 615-889-6700.

July 24–25: Opry-lympics. Children who visit Opryland are invited to participate in Olympic-style games such as discus throwing and the broad jump. Medals are awarded to the winners. Contact Opryland Customer Service, 2802 Opryland Drive, Nashville, TN 37214. Phone: 615-889-6700.

August 18–21: Opryland Clogging Championship. Hundreds of individuals and teams from across the country will compete for prizes doing traditional country clog dancing, which bears some resemblance to tap dancing, but more vigorous and without taps.

October 14–16: Happy Birthday to the Grand Ole Opry—celebrating its 68th year in 1993. More than 20,000 Opry fans celebrate the birthday each October. The three-day festival features autograph and photo sessions with Opry stars and special concerts. Contact the Grand Ole Opry ticket office, 615-889-3060.

October 23–24 and 30–31: Howl-O-Ween at Opryland. Trick-or-treating, special magic shows, and costumed employees add to these weekends at the park. Contact Opryland Customer Service, 2802 Opryland Drive, Nashville, TN 37214. Phone: 615-889-6700.

November 1–December 25: Country Christmas. The Opryland Hotel stages special musical events and caroling, an arts and crafts fair, and international foods. The display includes 1.4 million outdoor lights, seven miles of red ribbon and six miles of evergreen garland. Twenty-foot-tall "trees" of poinsettias deck the lobby, and the Conservatory is the site for giant snowflakes and mechanical figures in holiday attire. Contact "A Country Christmas," Opryland Hotel, 2800 Opryland Drive, Nashville, TN 37214. Phone: 615-872-0600.

November 20–December 31: Christmas at Opryland. This event in the theme park, which is open daily, features special decorations, lights, Christmas shopping, holiday meals, and seasonal entertainment. Contact Opryland Customer Service, 2802 Opryland Drive, Nashville, TN 37214. Phone: 615-889-6700.

Opryland's 1993 Schedule and Prices

Operating days:

March 27–April 25	Saturday, Sunday
April 2 and 9	Friday
April 30–May 16	Friday, Saturday, Sunday

May 21–September 6	Daily
September 10–26	Friday, Saturday, Sunday
October 2–31	Saturday, Sunday
Nov. 20–Dec. 31	Daily

Hours are 10 A.M. to 9 P.M. every day Opryland is open.

1993 Admission

* $22.95 is the one-day, one-price admission to all Opryland rides and shows for everyone age 12 and older.
* $34.95 is the two-day, one-price admission for two consecutive days.
* $12.95 is the one-day, one-price admission for children ages 4–11.
* $19.95 is the two-day, one-price admission for children ages 4–11 for two consecutive days.
* Children age 3 and younger are admitted free.
* The Opryland Passport: For $73.95, visitors get admission to Opryland for three consecutive days; a ticket to a Grand Ole Opry matinee, a day cruise on the *General Jackson;* a Grand Ole Opry sightseeing tour; a single concert admis-

sion to the Chevrolet/Geo Celebrity Theater; and admission to "Nashville Now" (subject to availability).

Miscellaneous

Parking costs $3 a day. The park has a kennel where you can leave Fido for $1 per day.

BUDGET ALERT!! Tickets are nonrefundable. In other words, check the weather forecast before you buy your tickets. Bring a foldable plastic poncho just in case.

MUSIC ROW ATTRACTIONS

Music Row got its name from the major recording studios clustered in this part of town. Within this four-block area, a great deal of country music is written, produced, published or recorded. Porter Wagoner Enterprises, Music Artists Corp., Warner Brothers, RCA, and CBS Records are among the businesses centered here. Watch for stars on their way to recording sessions!

The attractions here are open daily year-round unless otherwise noted. From downtown Nashville take Broadway west to 13th Avenue South and turn left. Take the first right, Demonbreun, and follow it to the heart of this area.

Barbara Mandrell Country: If you're a big fan of the honey-haired singer, you'll enjoy seeing her wedding dress, high school photos, and the model of her bedroom. June through August, 8 A.M. to 8 P.M. September through May, 9 A.M. to 5 P.M. Admission: $6.50; children under 12, $2.50. Address: 1510 Division Street. Phone: 615-242-7800.

Car Collectors Hall of Fame: A nice collection of classic models, including Elvis Presley's 1976 Cadillac Eldorado, Marty Robbins's 1934 Packard, a 1982 Buick convertible built for Tammy Wynette, and a 1981 DeLorean, the world's only stainless steel car. June through August, 8 A.M. to 8 P.M.; September through May, 9 A.M. to 5 P.M. Admission: $4.95; children under 12, $3.25. Address: 1534 Demonbreun Street. Phone: 615-255-6804.

DON'T MISS!! *Country Music Hall of Fame and Museum:* The definitive collection of country music memorabilia. Costumes, rare musical instruments, photos, and Elvis Presley's "Solid Gold Cadillac." There also is a display of hit songs scribbled on napkins, hotel stationery, even a real estate form—a reminder that the best ideas may have sprung from sudden inspiration. Included in the admission is a visit to RCA's Studio B, where stars like Elvis and Dolly recorded their early hits. June through August, open daily 8 A.M. to 7 P.M.; Sundays, 9 A.M. to 5 P.M. September through May, open daily 9 A.M. to 5 P.M. Admission: $7.50; children under 12, $2. Address: 4 Music Square East. Phone: 615-256-1639.

Country Music Wax Museum and Mall: More than sixty wax figures of country stars in original stage costumes. Several shops in the mall including the Willie Nelson and Family General Store. June through August, 9 A.M. to 8 P.M.; September through May, 9 A.M. to 5 P.M. Admission to the museum: $4; children under 12, $1.75. Address: 118 16th Avenue South. Phone: 615-256-2490.

Elvis Presley Museum: More than 400 artifacts of "The King," including a 1969 six-door Mercedes, guns, jewelry, furniture, guitars, and clothing. May through September, 9 A.M. to 9 P.M.; October through April, open Sundays through Thursdays, 9 A.M. to 6 P.M., Fridays and Saturdays, 9 A.M. to 8 P.M. Admission: $4; children under 12, $3. Address: 1520 Demonbreun Street. Phone: 615-256-8311.

Hank Williams Jr. Museum: Memorabilia from Williams Jr. and Sr. includes Hank Sr.'s '52 Cadillac, stage costumes, guitars, guns, and some rare photos. March through September, 8 A.M. to 9 P.M.; October through February, 8 A.M. to 3 P.M. Admission: $4; children under 16 free when ac-

companied by an adult. Address: 1524 Demonbreun Street. Phone: 615-242-8313.

Jim Owens Studio: The syndicated television
show "Crook and Chase," starring Lorianne
Crook (Mrs. Jim Owens) and Charlie Chase is
taped here. Tapings Monday through Friday at 7
P.M. are free and open to the public. Reservations are required. Address: 1525 McGavock.
Phone: 615-256-7700; or call the Nashville Network reservation office at 615-883-7000.

Recording Studios of America: You too can cut a
record. For $12.95 a technician will guide you as
you sing along with a prerecorded 24-track background. Lots of recordings from which to select,
including "Happy Birthday." Plenty of practice
time in a private booth. Videos also can be made
of your singing debut. June through August, 8
A.M. to 8 P.M.; September through May, 9 A.M. to
5 P.M. Address: 1510 Division Street. Phone: 615-
254-1282; 800-745-0296.

*Upper Room Chapel and Museum and Agape Gar-
den:* This interesting museum has a wood carving
of da Vinci's *The Last Supper* by Ernest Pelligrini
as well as other religious artifacts and old manu-
scripts. No admission charge. The garden is
lovely. Mondays through Saturdays 8 A.M. to 4:30
P.M. Address: 1908 Grand Avenue. Phone: 615-
340-7207.

MUSIC VALLEY DRIVE

In addition to Opryland theme park, this area northeast of downtown is home to several other country music attractions. From downtown, take I-40 to Briley Parkway. Music Valley attractions are near Exit 12B.

Belle Carol Riverboat Company: The 250-passenger *Captain Ann* and 400-passenger *Music City Queen* offer daytime sightseeing cruises on the Cumberland and dinner/entertainment cruises in the evening. A five-hour tour, complete with historical commentary, departs from the Music Valley dock and cruises to downtown Nashville. Passengers disembark at Riverfront Park for two hours of sightseeing downtown, then reboard the steamboat for the return trip. The trip can be made in reverse: from downtown the boat drops passengers at the Music Valley dock to sightsee in that area before the return voyage. There's also a 2½-hour boat cruise. Admission: $9.25; children under 12, $6.50. The prime rib dinner/entertainment cruise costs $30.80 for adults; children under 12, $19.50. A Sunday Brunch cruise is $15.75; children under 12, $10.95. And there are party cruises on Fridays and Saturdays from 10 P.M. to 1 A.M. Dancing to a live band, and a cash bar. For adults only. Phone: 615-244-3430; 800-342-2355.

Cars of the Stars: A large collection with some models that belonged to famous people, as well as street rods and other interesting models. Daily, 8 A.M. to 9 P.M. Admission: $4; children 12 and under, $2. Address: 2611 McGavock Pike. Phone: 615-885-7400.

Marty Robbins Memorial Showcase: Highlights of Robbins's long career including three personal cars, his NASCAR racer, and many awards. Address: 2613 McGavock Pike. Phone: 615-885-1515.

Music Valley Wax Museum of the Stars: More than fifty lifelike figures of country music greats in original costumes. Lots of memorabilia. May 28–September 3, daily from 8 A.M. to 9 P.M.; September 4–May 27, 9 A.M. to 5 P.M. Admission: $4; children under 12, $2. Address: 2515 McGavock Pike. Phone: 615-883-3612.

Nashville Toy Museum: More than 150 toy and model boats along with lots of trains, dolls, and bears. May 28 to September 3, 8 A.M. to 9 P.M.; rest of year, 9 A.M. to 5 P.M. Admission: $3.50; children under 12, $1.50. Address: 2613 McGavock Pike. Phone: 615-883-8870.

OTHER ATTRACTIONS

In addition to the venues listed here of interest
to devotees of country music, Nashville has
other attractions if you have time to see them.
The Tennessee Botanical Gardens, Vanderbilt
Fine Arts Gallery, the Cumberland Science Museum, and the Nashville Zoo are each worth the
time.

Belle Meade Plantation: Seven miles southwest of
downtown, this 1853 Greek Revival mansion
was the center of a 5400-acre plantation, highly
reputed as a thoroughbred horse farm. Now, the
mansion, carriage house, and other buildings
make a peaceful place to wander or have a picnic
lunch. Open Mondays through Saturdays 9 A.M.
to 5 P.M.; Sundays, 1 to 5 P.M. Admission: $5;
children 13–18, $3.50; 6–12, $2. Address: 5025
Harding Road. Phone: 615-356-0501.

Belmont Mansion: Three miles southwest of
downtown, this 1850s Italian villa was built by
Adelicia Acklen, one of the wealthiest women in
the United States at that time. It's noted for its
gardens, statuary, paintings, and elegant furnishings. Admission: $4; children under 12, $2. June
through August, Mondays through Saturdays, 10
A.M. to 4 P.M.; Sundays, 2 to 5 P.M.; September
through May, Tuesdays through Saturdays, 10

A.M. to 4 P.M. Address: 1900 Belmont Blvd.
Phone: 615-269-9537.

The Hermitage: President Andrew Jackson's
home, twelve miles northeast of downtown, is
worth the drive. The Greek Revival house on
625 acres was rebuilt in 1836 after fire destroyed
the first house on that site. The Hermitage is
furnished almost entirely with the family's original purchases. The gardens of the mansion are
beautiful and restful. In the visitors' center,
guests find information about the seventh president's life. The tour is self-guided, and visitors
listen to dramatizations of the voices of Jackson
and household members. On the grounds is a
restaurant, gift shops, picnic grove, and free
parking. Accessible to those with disabilities.
Open daily 9 A.M. to 5 P.M., except Thanksgiving,
Christmas, and the third week in January. Admission: $7; children under 18, $3.50; under 6,
free. Address: 4580 Rachel's Lane. Four miles
north of I-40 Exit 221 to Old Hickory Boulevard.
Phone: 615-889-2941.

DON'T MISS!! *House of Cash:* A wonderful collection of memorabilia from Johnny Cash, June
Carter Cash, and the Carter Family. Included
are Johnny's "One Piece at a Time" Cadillac,
made up of parts dating from 1949 to 1973.
Childhood portraits, Remington bronzes, and

hundreds of awards are among the items of interest. Open the first weekend in April through the first weekend in November, Mondays through Saturdays, 9 A.M. to 4:30 P.M. Admission: $6; children under 12, free. Address: 700 Johnny Cash Parkway, Hendersonville. Phone: 615-824-5110.

DON'T MISS!! While you're out in Hendersonville, take a drive by Johnny and June's lovely home on Hickory Lake. From the House of Cash, turn left on Johnny Cash Parkway, then right on Caudhill Drive. They live about a mile on the right, natural wood with a stone and rail fence. There's a guard house in front, an American flag in the side yard.

Jim Reeves Museum: Six miles northeast of downtown, this historic house, built in 1794, houses lots of personal items including Reeves's bedroom furniture, gold records, costumes, and his tour bus. Open daily 9 A.M. to 5 P.M. Admission: $4; children under 12, $2. Address: 1023 Joyce Lane, off Briley Parkway at exit 14B. Phone: 615-226-2062.

Kitty Wells/Johnny Wright Family Country Junction: Five miles north of downtown, this museum features memorabilia from the pair's fifty-four years in show business. Mondays through Saturdays, 9 A.M. to 5 P.M. No admission charge. Address: 240 Old Hickory Blvd. Phone: 615-865-9118.

The Nashville Network: Nine miles northeast of downtown, this international cable television station gives visitors a chance to see programs in production. Mondays through Fridays, join the audience of "Nashville Now," a live ninety-minute interview and performance show hosted by Ralph Emery. Admission is $5. Reservations required; call 615-889-6611. Other programs produced before an audience include "On Stage," a concert show; "Country Kitchen," a cooking program; "Crook and Chase," a talk show; and "Top Card," a game show. Address: 2806 Opryland Drive. For show schedules, call 615-883-7000.

DON'T MISS!! *Ryman Auditorium:* This is where country music began for Nashville. From 1943 to 1974, every Saturday night, this hall was the broadcast location for the Grand Ole Opry. The 3000-seat Union Gospel Tabernacle, complete with wooden pews and stained-glass windows, was built by riverboat captain Tom Ryman. Later it became Nashville's municipal auditorium and saw many famous actors grace the stage. Now, it's a little sad to see it empty, but heartwarming to recall the many country stars like Roy Acuff, Little Jimmy Dickens, and Minnie Pearl, who got their shot at fame in this hall. Open daily 8:30 A.M. to 4:30 P.M. Admission: $2.50; children under 12, $1.

Twitty City: Across from the House of Cash, go through Conway Twitty's high-tech museum before beginning a tour of the first floor of Twitty's private home in a nine-acre walled complex. When Twitty's in town, he often comes downstairs to meet the visitors. Open daily 9 A.M. to 5 P.M. Admission: $8; children under 12, $4.50. From November 22 to December 31, the grounds are atwinkle with more than a half-million lights and fifty lighted displays; open 5 to 9 P.M. Admission: $6.50; children under 12, $3. Music Village Boulevard, Hendersonville. Phone: 615-882-6650.

COUNTRY MUSIC NIGHTLIFE

For live performances by country musicians, there are several clubs from which to choose. Also see the section on Opryland, because the Grand Ole Opry is listed there, as are clubs inside Opryland Hotel.

The Bluebird Cafe: Six miles west of downtown, this spot features live music with up-and-coming artists and songwriters. The club is to be featured in an upcoming Hollywood movie, titled *The Thing Called Love,* directed by Peter Bogdanovich. Writer's night on Sundays; open mike night Mondays. Cover charge after 9 P.M. Reservations recommended at this small, popular cafe. Address: 4104 Hillsboro Road. Phone: 615-383-1461.

Boots Randolph's: In the old downtown historic district, "Mr. Yakety Sax" performs show Tuesdays through Saturdays at 9 P.M. Be sure to call for a performance schedule, as Randolph tours several weeks a year. There is a $9.50 cover charge for the show. Dinner is optional. See details in the *Dining* section. Address: 209 Printer's Alley. Phone: 615-256-5500.

The Captain's Table: Near Boots Randolph's, this supper club offers four shows nightly. Open Mondays through Saturdays. Happy hour, 4 to 6 P.M. Dinner served from 6 to 11:30 P.M. Dinner prices range from $10.95 to $17.95. Shows at 7, 8:30, and 10 P.M.; late show (no dinner) at 11:30 P.M. Reservations recommended. Address: 313 Church Street at the entrance to Printer's Alley. Phone: 615-251-9535; 615-256-3353.

Ernest Tubb Record Shop Midnight Jamboree: Near Opryland, this club offers live performances in the Grand Ole Opry format. Opry stars as well as newcomers perform. Shows every Saturday night at midnight. Guests need to arrive by 11:30 P.M. No cover charge. Address: 2414 Music Valley Drive. Phone: 615-889-2474.

Jim Ed Brown Theater: Grand Ole Opry star Jim Ed Brown does his hits "Three Bells," "Scarlet Ribbons," and more, nightly at 7 P.M. from March 27 through mid-December. Joining him is Sheb Wooley, known for his 1960 hit song, "The Purple People Eater." Wooley also appeared on television's "Rawhide" as Pete Nolan. The two-hour music and comedy show in the 480-seat theater costs $12; children under 12, $8. The theater also hosts "Breakfast with the Stars." For $10, visitors get to chow down with a country star or two at 7:30 A.M. Mondays through Fridays. Located near the Opryland Hotel, take exit 12B off Briley Parkway. Address: 2620 Music Valley Drive. Phone: 615-885-5701.

Nashville Nightlife: Live country entertainment nightly from 6 P.M. to 1 A.M. Large dance floor. Cover charge: $4. Address: 2620 Music Valley Drive. Phone: 615-885-5701.

Nashville Palace: Live entertainment nightly at 9 P.M. October through April, Sundays through Thursdays at 8 P.M. Often features Grand Ole Opry stars. This is where singer Randy Travis got his big break. Call to check cover charge. Address: 2400 Music Valley Drive. Phone: 615-885-1540.

Pennington's: This lounge in the Ramada Inn across from the Opryland Hotel features live country entertainment nightly. Address: 2800 Opryland Drive. Phone: 615-889-1000.

Starwood Amphitheatre: Ten miles southeast of downtown, this 17,000-seat amphitheater books popular music stars from pop to rock 'n' roll to country. About once a month a major country star performs during the season from May through October. Five thousand seats are under a roof, with the rest of the seating on the grass. Tentatively scheduled for 1993 are Hank Williams Jr., Clint Black, Travis Tritt, George Strait, and Alabama. Often, the Hank Williams Jr. concert is around Memorial Day. The Travis Tritt concert may be scheduled for July 4. For exact dates and ticket reservations, call Ticketmaster at 1-800-333-4849. Admissions vary depending on the artist, but range from $10 for a lawn seat to $25 for "Golden Circle" seats in the first ten rows of seats. For viewing the concerts from the lawn, lawn chairs are available to rent, or you may bring a blanket. Address: 3839 Murfreesboro Road, Antioch, TN 37013. Phone: 615-641-5800.

Stock-Yard Bull Pen Lounge: Live country entertainment and dancing. Open nightly 7:30 P.M. to 2 A.M. Address: 901 Second Avenue and Stock Yard Blvd., downtown. Phone: 615-255-6464.

DON'T MISS!! *Tootsie's Orchid Lounge:* This old downtown bar has a rich history reflected on the walls, papered in photos and memorabilia from the many country stars who spent time at Tootsie's. With its back entrance across the alley from the back door of the Ryman Auditorium, it was a favorite place for entertainers to catch a drink between performances on the Grand Ole Opry. Some had to be rousted from Tootsie's and hurried onstage for their performances. Old-timers and newcomers perform in this small club from noon to midnight daily. Don't expect anything fancy. This is the authentic old country music scene—and it has a charm all its own. Address: 422 Broadway. Phone: 615-726-3739.

BREAKING INTO THE NASHVILLE MUSIC SCENE

An executive with one of Nashville's top music publishers says that while there are no closed doors in the industry, most publishing houses are already so busy that it's a good idea to have an introduction from someone else before you knock on their front door. Here are some agencies that can help with that initial contact. These organizations have "writer relations" departments that will listen.

A spokesman with the Nashville Songwriters Association said a staff of six tries to keep up with the tapes aspiring writers drop off. "We try to make time because you never know who the next great writer will be," he said.

Nashville Songwriters' Association International: 1 Music Square West, Nashville, TN 37203. 615-256-3354.

BMI: Broadcast Music, Inc. 10 Music Square East, Nashville, TN 37203. 615-244-0044; 800-326-4264.

ASCAP: 2 Music Square West, Nashville, TN 37203. 615-742-5000.

Country Music Association, Inc.: One Music Circle South, Nashville, TN 37203. 615-244-2840.

Sesac, Inc.: 55 Music Square East, Nashville, TN 37203. 615-320-0055.

A tip from the professionals is to get all the exposure you can. "Sing everywhere they'll listen and keep trying," is Louise Mandrell's advice.

The Bluebird Cafe, 4104 Hillsboro Road, Nashville, is one place to do that. It's the best-known establishment among several other Nashville clubs that have "writer's night." Every Monday and Thursday, writers show up at the small café at 5:30 P.M. and put their names in a hat. Twenty-five names are drawn and each songwriter performs one number during the show, which runs from 6 to 9 P.M. Writers whose names weren't drawn get to perform at the next writer's night.

Café owner Amy Kurland said some music publishers and managers regularly attend writer's nights, but she said it would be naive to think that you can get a contract signed for a song after one performance. For most, it's a matter of playing on a lot of writer's nights and getting known around town. Performers who stand out on writer's night may be booked on the early shows on weeknights and have a thirty-minute slot to showcase their talent.

Kurland said the café also receives about a hundred tapes a month from songwriters. The staff listens to all of them and will contact writers who seem promising. For more information, write The Bluebird Cafe, 4104 Hillsboro Road, Nashville, TN 37215. Phone: 615-383-1461.

Particularly for performers, there's another possible break-in arena in Nashville. Opryland USA sponsors an annual talent search for its cast of more than 800 people in 25 live musical shows. They look for singers, dancers, actors, conductors, instrumentalists, stage managers, crew members, and costume dressers.

Opryland offers seminars on acting and vocal technique as well as dance classes. They offer internship programs that provide three to six hours of transferable elective credit hours through several universities.

They also produce more than 1000 convention and trade shows nationally, as well as the programs on the Nashville Network.

Opryland representatives hold auditions in more than forty cities across the country. Singers need to prepare at least three vocal selections, instrumentalists are asked to sight-read, and dancers need to prepare a one-minute sample of their best style. Auditions also are held for actors, strolling entertainers, and stage managers. Interviews for technicians and costume dressers are held in Nashville. The salary scale ranges from $220 to more than $600 a week.

* A piano accompanist (bring your own music) or cassette player is furnished.
* Auditions are for jobs at Opryland in Nashville and Fiesta Texas in San Antonio. These auditions are not for the Nashville Network or the Grand Ole Opry.
* You must be at least sixteen years old to work.

For information on where and when auditions will be held, write: Auditions USA, Room 900, 2802 Opryland Drive, Nashville, TN 37214. Call 800-94-STAGE.

SHOPPING

Shopping's great in Nashville. Don't let the eight large malls wear you out, because there are wonderful and unusual shops in the historic downtown section. And you won't be able to overlook the gift shops at every attraction and country music museum. That's because marketing experts designed the venues so that visitors exit through the gift shops.

The malls are generally open Mondays through Saturdays from 10 A.M. to 9:30 P.M., and Sundays from 1 to 6 P.M. Here's the rundown:

Bellevue Center: More than 120 stores, including Abercrombie and Fitch, Banana Republic, and Godiva Chocolatier; anchored by Dillard's and Castner Knott. In southwest Nashville at the Bellevue exit from I-40 West. Phone: 615-646-8690.

Church Street Centre: Three levels of shopping in 54 boutiques downtown; anchored by The Limited. A food court and full-service restaurant. Open Mondays through Saturdays 10 A.M. to 8 P.M. Phone: 615-256-6644.

Cool Springs Galleria: Located in tony Brentwood, an area southwest of downtown where lots of celebrities have homes, this complex has 100 shops, restaurants, and a ten-screen theater; anchored by Dillard's, Sears, and Castner Knott. Address: 1800 Galleria Blvd., off I-65 at Moores Lane. Phone: 615-771-2050.

Green Hills Mall: More than 80 shops, including The Nature Company, Laura Ashley, and Williams & Sonoma; anchored by Dillard's, Castner Knott, Gus Mayer, and Walgreen. Located at Hillsboro and Abbot Martin roads, southwest of downtown. Phone: 615-298-5478.

Harding Mall: Sixty shops, including two major department stores and a six-screen theater; anchored by Castner Knott and Marshall's. Located at Harding Place and Nolensville Pike, southeast of downtown. Phone: 615-833-6327.

Hickory Hollow Mall: Anchored by Castner Knott, Sears, J.C. Penney, and Dillard's; 180 specialty shops. Located at Exit 60 off I-24 East, southeast of downtown. Phone: 615-731-4500.

Madison Square Shopping Center: Thirty-eight stores and two restaurants; anchored by Walgreen, Woolworth, Western Auto, and Peebles. Located on Gallatin Pike near Briley Parkway, north of Opryland. Phone: 615-860-2131.

Rivergate Mall: Castner Knott, Dillard's, J.C. Penney, and Sears anchor this 164-shop mall. There's a food court and four restaurants. Located at Exit 96 off I-65 North, north of Opryland. Phone: 615-859-3458.

Specialty Shops: Looking for a hard-to-find recording? If you don't find it in one of these shops, it probably doesn't exist:

Conway's Twitty Bird Record Shop: 1530 Demonbreun Street. Phone: 615-242-2466.

Ernest Tubb Record Shops: Three locations: 2414 Music Valley Drive, 615-889-2474; 417 Broadway, 615-255-7503; 1516 Demonbreun Street, 615-244-2845.

Tower Records: 2400 West End Ave. Phone: 615-327-3722.

Need some cowboy duds?

Boot Hill: 315 West Trinity Lane. Take I-65 North to Exit 87B. 615-227-3600.

Loretta Lynn's Western Stores: On Music Row at the corner of 16th Avenue and Demonbreun Street. Phone: 615-256-2814.

The Nashville Cowboy: 118 16th Avenue South. 615-242-9497.

Want to find the unusual?

DON'T MISS!! *Dangerous Threads:* This shop has truly amazing fashions for men and women, from leather chaps with rhinestones to spandex satin dresses with fringe. Footwear and jewelry too. Open Mondays through Saturdays, 10 A.M. to 7 P.M.; closed Sundays. Two locations: 2201 Elliston Place, near Vanderbilt University, 615-320-5890; downtown at 105 Second Ave., 615-256-1033.

Karma: This downtown shop has a great selection of T-shirts, crystals, incense, posters—even ultratrendy Dr. Marten shoes. Open Mondays through Thursdays, 10 A.M. to 8 P.M.; Fridays and Saturdays, 10 A.M. to 10 P.M.; Sundays, 1 to 7 P.M. Address: 168 Second Ave. Phone: 615-726-2015.

Other nifty places:

Botanical Warehouse: This downtown warehouse sells plants of all shapes and sizes. It also rents them by the day, week, month, or year. AND, it rents bicycles by the day or hour too. Open Mondays through Saturdays, 10 A.M. to 5 P.M.; closed Sundays. Address: 124 Second Avenue. Phone: 615-244-3915.

Davis-Kidd Booksellers: If bookstores soothe you, this is paradise, with more than 250,000 volumes. Open Mondays through Thursdays, 9:30 A.M. to 9 P.M.; Fridays and Saturdays, 9:30 A.M. to 11 P.M.; Sundays, noon to 6 P.M. Address: 4007 Hillsboro Road. Phone: 615-385-2645.

Farmers Market: Open year-round on weekends, this is a great flea market, and offers fresh fruits, vegetables, and plants as well. Located at 618 Jackson Street between Seventh and Eighth avenues North. Phone: 615-862-6765.

Greenleaf: A shop inside the Opryland Hotel complex that specializes in bonsai trees. Everything you need to get started, along with beautiful specimens of the Japanese art of miniature trees. Open daily from 9 A.M. to 9 P.M. Address: 2800 Opryland Drive. Phone: 615-889-1000, ext. 2866.

The Nashville Arcade: Connecting Fourth and Fifth avenues North, this two-tiered array of shops opened in 1903.

DINING

Eating out is fun in Nashville, with the variety and ethnicity inherent to cities. Visitors can choose from places easy on the budget, to special-occasion dinners never to be forgotten. And there are the old-time local favorites where, once you taste the food and revel in the ambience, you'll understand why they're standouts.

Unless otherwise noted, these restaurants are open year-round, take major credit cards, and are accessible to the disabled.

BUDGET ALERT!! *Belle Meade Cafeteria:* Four miles southwest of downtown, this is traditional southern cooking with reasonable prices. It's been a local favorite for years. Open daily for lunch 11 A.M. to 2 P.M.; dinner, 4:30 to 8 P.M. Address: 4534 Harding Road in Belle Meade Plaza. Phone: 615-298-5571.

DON'T MISS!! *The Bluebird Cafe:* Three miles west of downtown. Not only is the food fine, it's known for nightly live entertainment. Recommended by country singer Kathy Mattea. Open daily for dinner, 5:30 P.M. to 11 P.M. After 9 P.M. there's a cover charge for the entertainment. Reservations recommended. Ask to be on the mailing list for upcoming special events. The 10th anniversary bash in 1992 drew old friends of the Bluebird like Pam Tillis, Nanci Griffith, and Don Henry. Address: 4101 Hillsboro Road. Phone: 615-383-1461.

Boots Randolph's: Downtown at 209 Printer's Alley, the sax man himself entertains at 9 P.M. shows Mondays through Saturdays. Dinner with the show ranges from $10.95 to $25.95. Reservations required for dinner. Phone: 615-256-5500.

Broadway Dinner Train: A four-course dinner with your choice of three entrees, served in restored dining cars during a 2½-hour train ride 35 miles toward Old Hickory and back. The route was once part of the Tennessee Central Railway and is now owned by the Nashville and Eastern Railroad. After dinner, sit in the dome car and enjoy the view and cocktail service. Boards Thursdays through Saturdays at 6:30 P.M. Summer schedule may expand. It's $39.95 per person; reservations required. Not equipped to accommodate wheelchairs. First Avenue South and Broadway at Riverfront Park, downtown. Phone: 615-254-8000.

BUDGET ALERT!! *Country Star Cafe:* On Music Row, this café offers good food that's cheap. From 8 to 10:30 A.M. daily you can get two eggs, sausage or bacon, with biscuits or toast, for $1.89. At lunch try chicken and dumplings with corn bread for $1.79. And the walls are lined with old photos of country music stars. Look for a photo of Paul Anka with a full head of hair. Open Sundays through Thursdays, 8 A.M. to 6 P.M.; Fridays and Saturdays to 7 P.M. Address: 1528 Demonbreun Avenue. Phone: 615-254-5400.

Crawdaddy's: Try the Cajun-style seafood entrees at this downtown spot. Open Monday through Friday for lunch, 11 A.M. to 2 P.M.; Mondays through Saturdays for dinner from 5 P.M. Sundays, try Brunch with Jazz for $16.95. Reservations recommended. Address: 14 Oldham Street. Phone: 615-255-5434.

Gerst Haus: One mile east of downtown, have fun with a German band while you sample the schnitzel. Open for lunch and dinner Mondays through Saturdays from 11 A.M. to 10 P.M.; Sundays, noon to 10 P.M. Address: 228 Woodland Street. Phone: 615-256-9760.

DON'T MISS!! *Ichiban Japanese Restaurant and Sushi Bar:* This downtown restaurant attracts a lot of Japanese diners. That's a good sign. Try the complete dinner: soup, salad, entrée, and five pieces of sushi (raw seafood) for $14.50. Or sit at the sushi bar and sample the crunchy shrimp or smelt roe. The menu boasts 99 appetizers. Open Mondays through Fridays, 11:30 A.M. to 2 P.M.; Mondays through Sundays for dinner, 5 to 10 P.M. Address: 109 Second Avenue North. Phone: 615-254-7185.

Jack's Bar-B-Que: Two locations for this great barbecued pork shoulder and ribs. They also have smoked turkey and chicken, and barbecued bologna! At the Riverfront Park location, 100 Broadway, it's take-out or eat on the patio. Open Sundays through Thursdays, 11 A.M. to 6 P.M.; Fridays and Saturdays, 11 A.M. to midnight. Phone: 615-354-5715. The northside location, 334 West Trinity Lane off I-65 north at exit 87B, has dine-in or drive-through facilities. Phone: 615-228-9888.

DON'T MISS!! *Kobe Steaks Japanese Restaurant:* This one's an experience to remember. Kobe beef is from cows raised in Japan, fattened on beer, and massaged for tender meat. A dozen diners are seated around the grill for a slicing and chopping extravaganza by the chef. Dinners range from $10.50 to $22.50 apiece. Open Sundays through Thursdays from 5 to 10:30 P.M.; Fridays and Saturdays until 11:30 P.M. Reservations recommended. Address: 210 25th Avenue North, three miles west of downtown. Phone: 615-327-9081.

Loveless Cafe: Fifteen miles southwest of downtown, this is a 35-year-old restaurant mentioned in *People* magazine because it's a favorite for Nashville celebrities. They go there for the country ham with red-eye gravy, biscuits with homemade blackberry preserves, and other southern traditions. Open Tuesdays through Saturdays 8 A.M. to 2 P.M., and 5 P.M. to 9 P.M.; Sundays, 8 A.M. to 9 P.M. Closed Mondays. Reservations recommended. Highway 100, Nashville. From I-40, take exit 192, turn left on McCrory Lane. Go four miles to Highway 100. Turn left, go 100 yards. Phone: 615-646-9700.

Mama Mia's Italian Restaurant: Eight miles southeast of downtown. Family-style Italian dining. Closed Sundays and Mondays. Open for dinner Tuesdays through Saturdays 5 to 10 P.M.

Dinners range from $5.95 to $18.95. Reservations recommended. Address: 4501 Trousdale Drive. Phone: 615-331-7207.

Mere Bulles: This charming downtown bistro offers continental cuisine. Open Monday through Friday from 11 A.M. to 3 P.M.; for dinner Sundays through Thursdays, 5:30 to 10 P.M.; Fridays and Saturdays until 11 P.M. Lunch ranges from $3.95 to $12.95; dinner from $8.95 to $21.95. Reservations required. Jazz entertainment begins at 5 P.M. Address: 152 Second Avenue. Phone: 615-256-1946.

New Orleans Manor: Five miles southeast of downtown, the Manor offers a seafood feast. An all-you-can-eat buffet of oysters, shrimp, herring, salmon, crab legs, clams, scallops, and more. Prime and barbecued ribs, soups, salads, and desserts. All this in an elegant southern mansion. Price per person: $27 to $34. Open Tuesdays through Saturdays from 5 P.M. Reservations recommended. Address: 1400 Murfreesboro Road. Phone: 615-367-2777.

Old Spaghetti Factory: This eclectic downtown joint is open for lunch from 11:30 A.M. to 2 P.M.; dinners from 5 to 10 P.M.; Sunday, 4 to 10 P.M. Italian treats range from $4.25 to $8.50. Address: 160 Second Avenue. Phone: 615-254-9010.

Rio Bravo Cantina: For a Tex-Mex taste, go two miles west of downtown. Open daily from 11 A.M. to 11 P.M. Dinner prices from $4 to $15. Address: 3015 West End Avenue. Phone: 615-329-1745.

BUDGET ALERT!! *San Antonio Taco Co.:* Kids under age ten eat free at the two locations of this casual restaurant. (Two children per adult.) For those over age 10, there's an extensive menu of Tex-Mex treats at low prices. Try a generous chicken enchilada plate with beans and rice for $4. Or a yummy guacamole taco for $1.15. Open Mondays through Thursdays, 11 A.M. to 9 P.M.; Fridays and Saturdays, 11 A.M. to midnight. Closed Sundays. Address: 208 Commerce Street downtown, 615-259-4413. And: 416 21st Avenue, 615-327-4322.

The Shack: If you're headed out toward Hendersonville, DON'T MISS!! a great selection of seafood, prime rib, and steaks from $7.95 to $25.95. While you wait, eat the free peanuts and throw the shells on the floor. Really. Open daily from 3 to 11 P.M., or later. Address: 2420 N. Gallatin Road between Opryland and Hendersonville. Phone: 615-859-9777.

DON'T MISS!! BUDGET ALERT!! *Shells:* The drive eight miles southeast of downtown is worth the trip for the delicious seafood at reasonable prices in a casual atmosphere. Try a pound of Shrimp Scampi served with a loaf of fresh bread for $8.45. And for those of us whose favorite food is raw oysters on the half shell, this is heaven for $2.95 a dozen. Steaks and chicken for landlubbers. Open Mondays through Thursdays, 11 A.M. to 10 P.M.; Fridays until 11 P.M.; Saturdays, 5 to 11 P.M.; Sundays, 11 A.M. to 9 P.M. Address: 1210 Murfreesboro Road. Phone: 615-399-1495.

DON'T MISS!! *Stock-Yard Restaurant:* For extraordinary steak, try this downtown restaurant, long a favorite with area residents and visitors. After dinner, visit the Bull Pen Lounge from 8:30 P.M. to 2 A.M. daily. Live entertainment and occasional surprise visits from well-known celebrities. Try "Tennessee Tea," a drink made with nine liquors and served in a souvenir mug. Open for lunch Mondays through Fridays, 11 A.M. to 2 P.M.; open for dinner daily, 5 to 11 P.M. Dinners range from $12.50 to $27.50. Reservations recommended. Address: 901 Second Avenue. Phone: 615-255-6464.

The Toucan Restaurant: The emphasis in this trendy café is on light, healthy, and creative foods with influences from California and the Caribbean. Try grilled salmon with black bean relish in tequila lime sauce. You may want to dine on the patio or upper veranda. In the Music

Row area. Dinners range from $7 to $14. Open
Mondays through Fridays, 11 A.M. to 11 P.M.; Saturdays, 5 to 11 P.M. Closed Sundays. Reservations recommended. Address: 26 Music Square
East at 16th Avenue. Phone: 615-726-0101.

Union Station: Sunday brunch couldn't be more
charming than beneath the vaulted stained-glass
ceiling of the elegantly restored railroad station.
Champagne, omelettes made to order, smoked
salmon, are some of the treats. From 11 A.M. to 2
P.M. Reservations required. Adults, $14.95; chil-
dren under 12, $6.95. Address: 1001 Broadway.
Phone: 615-726-1001; 800-331-2123.

BUDGET ALERT!! *White Castle:* For those who
know and love these silver-dollar-sized ham-
burgers, there are five locations in Nashville.
Check a phone book for the closest locations.
Open 24 hours a day every day. Prices range
from 37 cents (for a White Castle burger) to $2.

The Wild Boar: And now for something com-
pletely different! The feature here is wild game
such as rabbit, boar, elk, or quail. And talk about
fresh fish . . . select a live fish or lobster from a
tank in the dining room. The menu includes
more standard fare as well. Dinners range from
$15 to $26. Buffalo rib-eye is $23.50. Open Mon-
days through Fridays for lunch, 11 A.M. to 2 P.M.;
Mondays through Saturdays for dinner, 5 to 10

P.M. Closed Sundays. Address: 2014 Broadway. Phone: 615-329-1313.

DON'T MISS!! BUDGET ALERT!! *Windows on the Cumberland:* This is a great, funky, downtown, upstairs, wood-floored place looking over the river. Monday through Wednesday, 11 A.M. to 3 P.M.; Thursdays and Fridays, 11 A.M. to 8 P.M.; Saturdays, noon to 8 P.M.; Sundays, 2 to 7 P.M. Try the homemade soup and a peanut butter, banana, and honey sandwich for $2.25. Or the manager's special: steamed veggies with red beans and rice, $4.50. Address: 112 Second Avenue. Phone: 615-244-7944.

CALENDAR OF EVENTS, 1993

Note: For a calendar of annual events at Opryland USA, check the Opryland USA listings.

January

Jan. 3: Twelfth Night Festival. Historic Travellers' Rest, the home of Judge John Overton five miles south of downtown, is the earliest restoration in Nashville, built in 1799. Candlelight tours, period music and dance, and special foods like syllabub and mulled wine. Historic Travel-

lers' Rest, 636 Farrell Parkway, Nashville, TN
37204. Phone: 615-832-2962.

Jan. 6–10: Nashville Boat and Sport Show. Boats,
recreation products, and fishing seminars draw
visitors to the Nashville Convention Center
downtown. For information, contact National
Marine Manufacturers Association, 1139 Ol-
livette Parkway, St. Louis, MO 63132. Phone:
314-567-0020.

February

Feb. 4–7: Antiques and Garden Show of Nashville. Beautifully landscaped display gardens
combine with more than fifty antique galleries
for this show in the downtown Convention Center. For information, contact Antiques and Garden Show of Nashville, 1200 Forest Park Drive,
Nashville, TN 37205. Phone: 615-352-1282.

Feb. 11–14: The Tennessee State Fairgrounds
just off I-65 is the site of a gathering of more
than 200 craftspeople. Includes demonstrations.
Contact Americana Sampler, Inc. P.O. Box
160009, Nashville, TN 37216. Phone: 615-227-
2080.

Feb. 12–13: Nashville Ballet Valentine's Series.
Repertoire performance of four ballets, including

one set to songs written by k.d. lang. Located downtown in Polk Theater. Contact Nashville Ballet, 2976 Sidco Drive, Nashville, TN 37204. Phone: 615-244-7233.

March

March 4–7: Southern Women's Show. The Convention Center downtown is host to more than 300 exhibits of interest to women, including food, fashions, jewelry, business, and travel. Contact Michelle Gibbons, Southern Shows, Inc. P.O. Box 36859, Charlotte, NC 28236. Phone: 704-376-6594.

March 28–April 1: Gospel Music Week. Downtown at the Convention Center and the Stouffer Hotel, five days of seminars, workshops, and concerts culminates with the 24th Annual Dove Awards on April 1. Contact Wendy Holt, Gospel Music Association, 7 Music Circle N., Nashville, TN 37203.

April

April 24–25: 10th Annual Main Street Festival. Fifteen miles south of downtown, the streets of Franklin fill with more than 250 craftspeople.

There's dancing in the streets, and children's rides and games. Contact Downtown Franklin Association, P.O. Box 807, Franklin, TN 37065. Phone: 615-790-7094.

May

May 3–9: Sara Lee Classic LPGA Gold Tournament. The Hermitage Golf Course in Old Hickory, 15 miles northwest of downtown, hosts 144 of the top women players in the world. Contact Clyde Russell, Sara Lee Classic, P.O. Box 390, Old Hickory, TN 37318. Phone: 615-847-5017.

May 7–9: 22nd Annual Tennessee Crafts Fair. The largest market of Tennessee crafts features 165 artists, live music, and ongoing craft demonstrations. In Centennial Park just west of downtown. Contact Tennessee Association of Craft Artists, P.O. Box 120066, Nashville, TN 37212. Phone: 615-665-0502.

May 15–16, 22–23, 29–31: Tennessee Renaissance Festival. Held in Triune, twenty miles south of downtown, this festival features jousting knights, medieval-style arts and food, even Gypsy jugglers. Contact Moore Entertainment, 615-320-9333.

June

June 3–6: Summer Lights Festival. The streets of downtown Nashville are the site for more than 120 entertainment acts from country to jazz. Contact Greater Nashville Arts Foundation, 400 Broadway, Nashville, TN 37203. Phone: 615-862-6720.

June 7–13: International Country Music Fan Fair. Held at the fairgrounds and Opryland, this week-long celebration offers more than 35 hours of stage shows along with picture and autograph sessions with country music stars. Contact Fan Fair, 2804 Opryland Drive, Nashville, TN 37214. Phone: 615-889-7503.

June 18–20: Bellevue Center Balloon Classic. More than sixty hot-air balloons color the skies of the park twenty miles southwest of downtown. Contact Main Event, Inc., P.O. Box 41250, Nashville, TN 37204. Phone: 615-255-2580.

July

July 4: Independence Day Celebration. Riverfront Park downtown is the site of food, fireworks, and music at this family-oriented, alcohol-free event. Contact Metro Parks, Cen-

tennial Park Office, Nashville, TN 37201.
Phone: 615-862-8400.

August

Aug. 6–8: Ninth Annual Americana Summer
Sampler Craft, Folk Art and Antique Fair. At the
state fairgrounds five miles south of downtown,
175 craftspeople and antique dealers gather.
Contact Americana Sampler, P.O. Box 160009,
Nashville, TN 37216. Phone: 615-227-2080.

September

Italian Street Fair. At the Maryland Farms Com-
plex in Brentwood, 15 miles south of downtown,
craftspeople, carnival rides, entertainment, and
Italian foods highlight this festival. Contact
Nashville Symphony Guild Office, Nashville,
TN 37204. Phone: 615-329-3033.

Sept. 11–12: Country Fair and Sunday Supper
on the grounds at Historic Travellers' Rest, five
miles south of downtown. Traditional crafts, period music, storytelling, and barbecue supper.
Contact Historic Travellers' Rest, 636 Farrell
Parkway, Nashville, TN 37204. Phone: 615-832-
8197.

Sept. 17–26: Tennessee State Fair. The fairgrounds just south of town offer rides, livestock and agriculture, crafts, antiques, and entertainment. Contact Tex Townsend, Tennessee State Fair, P.O. Box 40208, Nashville, TN 37204. Phone: 615-862-8980.

Sept. 18–19: 11th Annual African Street Festival. On the main campus of Tennessee State University, five miles west of downtown, join more than 100 merchants from 25 states; twelve exotic food concessions, and eight hours of stage shows including poetry, rap, reggae, blues, jazz, and gospel.

Sept. 18–19: Belle Meade Fall Fest. The grounds of the Belle Meade Plantation are the site of a "garage treasures sale," crafts, food, and children's activities. Contact Belle Meade Plantation, 5025 Harding Road, Nashville, TN 37205. Phone: 615-356-0501.

Sept. 27–Oct. 2: National Quartet Convention. The downtown Nashville Municipal Auditorium features more than 65 southern gospel artists in nightly concerts. Daytime activities include a Celebrity Roast, Talent Search, and seminars. Contact National Quartet Convention, 54 Music Square West, Nashville, TN 37203. Phone: 615-320-7000.

October

Oct. 2: Riverfest. Riverfront Park downtown is the site of music, food, and fireworks. Contact Nashville Area Junior Chamber of Commerce, 161 Fourth Avenue North, Nashville, TN 37219. Phone: 615-259-4750.

Oct. 9: 14th Annual Oktoberfest. In historic Germantown at the corner of Seventh Avenue North and Monroe Street, see strolling accordion players, polka dancing, crafts, and partake of German food. Contact Church of the Assumption, 1227 Seventh Avenue North, Nashville, TN 37208. Phone: 615-256-2729.

Oct. 22–24: Dunham's Station Rendezvous. For three days the Belle Meade Plantation grounds are the site of the re-creation of Tennessee Longhunter and Western Mountain Man camps. Activities include tomahawk throwing and black-powder rifle contests. Contact Belle Meade Plantation, 5025 Harding Road, Nashville, TN 37205. Phone: 615-356-0501.

November

Nov. 6–8: 8th Annual Americana Christmas Sampler Craft, Folk Art and Antique Fair. The state fairgrounds five miles south of downtown is host to 200 craftspeople and antique dealers from 25 states. Contact Americana Sampler, P.O. Box 160009, Nashville, TN 37216. Phone: 615-227-2080.

Nov. 12–14: Christmas Village. A three-day shopping event at the Tennessee State Fairgrounds, with more than 250 craftspeople and merchants. Santa's there too. Contact Christmas Village, P.O. Box 158826, Nashville, TN 37215.

Nov. 19–21: Longhorn World Championship Rodeo. At the downtown Nashville Municipal Auditorium, more than 250 of the country's best cowboys and cowgirls gather to compete for World Championship points. Bright costuming and lively music add to the pageantry. Contact Longhorn World Championship Rodeo, P.O. Box 70159, Nashville, TN 37207. Phone: 615-876-1016; 1-800-477-6336.

Nov. 27–Dec. 7: Christmas at Fox Hollow. In Franklin, fifteen miles south of downtown, Tom T. and Dixie Hall offer a festival with crafts, entertainment, and a tour of their home. At Moore's Lane Exit, four miles from I-65. Contact Animaland, 615-794-8679.

Nov. 27–Jan. 9: The Night Before Christmas. Belle Meade Plantation is lavishly decked out for a Victorian Christmas, featuring an exhibit of antique toys from the Detroit Historical Museum. Contact Belle Meade Plantation, 5025 Harding Road, Nashville, TN 37205. Phone: 615-356-0501.

December

Dec. 5–29: Trees of Christmas. The Tennessee Botanical Gardens and Fine Arts Center at Cheekwood, nine miles southwest of downtown, hosts cultural exhibits from many different countries. Contact Horticultural Society Office, 615-353-2150.

Dec. 11–12: 8th Annual Dickens of a Christmas. In Franklin, fifteen miles south of downtown, carolers in Victorian costumes, living windows of historic characters, strolling minstrels, street vendors, and hot wassail herald the season. Contact Downtown Franklin Association, P.O. Box 807, Franklin, TN 37065. Phone: 615-790-7094.

LODGING

Hotels/Motels

More than 125 hotels and motels offer visitors 20,000 rooms. And there's a wide range of prices from which to pick, ranging from the Interstate Inn near downtown Nashville ($34 for two people) to a room at the posh Opryland Hotel ($149 for two people).

BUDGET ALERT!! When you call for reservations, be sure to ask for the LOWEST RATE available for the dates of your visit. While room rates drop a bit in January and February, there's not much seasonal variation here.

Watch for:

★ lower weekend rates
★ special rates for visits of three days or more
★ higher rates if there's a special event in town (like the International Country Music Fan Fair in June)

Also:

★ Reservations are a good idea, especially during Fan Fair and from June through September.

* Rates given are for the 1993 season, but are subject to change. They do not include Nashville's 12.25 percent sales and room tax.
* Many hotels offer discounts to senior citizens.
* Many hotels do not charge extra for children under 12.
* Accommodations are open year-round, take major credit cards, and are equipped to accommodate disabled visitors, unless otherwise noted.
* Accommodations offer color TV with cable.
* Most lodgings do not accept pets.

Opryland Area

AmeriSuites: These 125 suites include continental breakfast and microwaves, outdoor pool, free parking, and shuttle service to the airport and to Opryland Hotel. Two people, $76 to $86. Address: 220 Rudy's Circle, Nashville, TN 37214. Phone: 615-872-0422; 800-833-1516.

Comfort Inn: This 121-unit motel has an outdoor pool and free parking. Two people, $39 to $69. Address: 2516 Music Valley Drive, Nashville, TN 37214. Phone: 615-889-0086; 800-228-5150.

Econo Lodge near Opryland: This 86-room motel has an outdoor pool, offers free parking, and allows pets. Two people, $37.95 to $59.95. Address: 2460 Music Valley Drive, Nashville, TN 37214. Phone: 615-889-0090; 800-446-6900.

Fiddlers Inn North: With 202 units, this motel has an outdoor pool and free parking. Two people, $34 to $59. Address: 2410 Music Valley Drive, Nashville, TN 37214. Phone: 615-885-1440.

DON'T MISS!! *Opryland Hotel:* Even if a stay here is beyond the budget, be sure to take a walk through this lavish and spectacular complex. See the section on Opryland USA for details. This 1891-room hotel offers 120 suites and 500 Garden Terrace rooms overlooking the tropical Cascades or the two-acre garden under the glass Conservatory. Tennis, swimming, an 18-hole golf course, shops, nine restaurants, and live entertainment lounges. They also have free parking. Two people, $159 to $189. Address: 2800 Opryland Drive, Nashville, TN 37214. Phone: 615-889-1000.

Park Inn International: An outdoor pool and a lounge with live entertainment compliments this 211-room motel. Two people, $44 to $65. Address: 2600 Music Valley Drive, Nashville, TN 37214. Phone: 615-889-8235; 800-388-3066.

Ramada Inn Across From Opryland: This 298-room hotel offers an indoor pool, free parking, shuttle service to the airport, and a lounge with darts and live entertainment. Two people, $60 to $96. Address: 2401 Music Valley Drive, Nashville, TN 37214. Phone: 615-889-0800.

Sheraton Music City Hotel: This 412-room hotel has indoor and outdoor pools, lighted tennis courts, a health club, and a lounge with live entertainment. Two people, $69 to $130. Address: 777 McGavock Pike, Nashville, TN 37214. Phone: 615-885-2200; 800-325-3535.

Shoney's Inn of Music Valley: These 185 rooms offer an indoor pool, free parking, and an airport shuttle service. Two people, $69 to $120. Address: 2420 Music Valley Drive, Nashville, TN 37214. Phone: 615-885-4030; 800-222-2222.

Downtown and Music Row Area

Best Western Metro Inn: This 147-unit hotel has a restaurant, outdoor pool, free parking, a shuttle to the airport, and allows pets. Two people, $36 to $55. Address: 99 Spring Street, Nashville, TN 37207. Phone: 615-259-9160.

Budget Host Inn: One hundred thirty units with an outdoor pool and free parking. Allows pets. Lounge with live entertainment. Two people,

$31.50 to $46. Address: 10 Interstate Drive, Nashville, TN 37213. Phone: 615-244-6050; 800-234-6779.

Days Inn Downtown: One hundred rooms include twenty nonsmoking rooms. Delicatessen and convenience market, free parking. Two people, $43 to $89. Address: 711 Union Street, Nashville, TN 37219. Phone: 615-242-4311; 800-251-1856.

Doubletree Hotel at Sovran Plaza: These 337 rooms include the use of an indoor pool. Two people, $89 to $119. Fourth Avenue North and Union Street, Nashville, TN 37239. Phone: 615-244-8200; 800-528-0444.

The Hermitage Hotel: With 112 suites, this elegant, classic hotel built in 1910 accepts small pets. Two people, $85 to $105. Address: 231 Sixth Avenue North, Nashville, TN 37219. Phone: 615-244-3121; 800-251-1908.

Holiday Inn Crowne Plaza: This 476-room hotel offers a lounge with live entertainment and indoor pool. Two people, $69 to $129. Address: 623 Union Street, Nashville, TN 37219. Phone: 615-259-2000.

Interstate Inn: With 84 rooms, this motel offers an outdoor pool, free parking, and they accept small pets. Address: 300 Interstate Drive, Nashville, TN 37213. Phone: 615-242-9621; 800-444-4401.

Quality Inn Hall of Fame: This 103-room hotel has an outdoor pool and offers free parking. Two people, $62. Address: 1407 Division Street, Nashville, TN 37203. Phone: 615-242-1631; 800-424-6423.

Ramada Inn Downtown: Guests in these 180 units have access to a lounge with live entertainment and a laundry room. Outdoor pool and free parking. Two people, $32 to $57. Address: 840 James Robertson Parkway, Nashville, TN 37203. Phone: 615-244-6130; 800-633-7108.

Regal Maxwell House Hotel: This lovely 289-room hotel features a lounge with live entertainment, health club, outdoor pool, free parking, and an airport shuttle. Two people, $89 to $109. Weekend rates, $59 to $79. Address: 2025 MetroCenter Blvd., Nashville, TN 37228. Phone: 615-259-4343; 800-457-4460.

Shoney's Inn of Nashville: With 147 rooms, there's an outdoor pool, free parking, one suite with an in-room Jacuzzi, and they accept pets. Two people, $59 to $89. Address: 1521 Demonbreun Street, Nashville, TN 37203. Phone: 615-255-9977; 800-222-2222.

Stouffer Nashville Hotel: This 673-room hotel offers complimentary coffee and newspaper, indoor pool, spa and health club, and they accept small pets. Two people, $150 to $190. Address: 611 Commerce Street, Nashville, TN 37203. Phone: 615-255-8400; 800-468-3571.

Union Station Hotel: A lovely, elegant place in the restored train station. The 127 rooms include a lounge with live entertainment. Some rooms open onto the high-ceiled interior of the station and include a complimentary terry bathrobe. Two people, $115 to $130. Address: 1001 Broadway, Nashville, TN 37203. Phone: 615-726-1001; 800-331-2123.

Other Locations

Budgetel Inn: Eight miles east of downtown, this 150-room motel has an outdoor pool and offers a complimentary continental breakfast. Shuttle service to the airport. Pets are allowed. Two people, $34.95 to $51.95. Address: 531 Donelson Pike at I-40, Nashville, TN 37214. Phone: 615-885-3100; 800-428-3438.

ClubHouse Inn: Six miles east of downtown, these 135 rooms offer a full complimentary breakfast and manager's reception daily. Indoor spa, outdoor pool, and an airport shuttle service. Two people, $66 to $82. Address: 2435 Atrium Way, Nashville, TN 37210. Phone: 615-880-0500; 800-258-2466.

Comfort Inn—Hermitage: Ten miles east of downtown, this 106-room motel has an outdoor pool. Rooms are available with waterbeds and whirlpool tubs. Two people, $35 to $65. I-40 at 5768 Old Hickory Blvd., Hermitage, TN 37076. Phone: 615-889-5060.

Comfort Suites: Eight miles east of downtown, this 50-suite hotel offers a complimentary breakfast buffet, outdoor pool, Jacuzzi and steam room, and airport shuttle service. Two people, $69 to $120. Address: 2615 Elm Hill Pike, Nashville, TN 37214. Phone: 615-883-0114; 800-445-1466.

Days Inn—Vanderbilt: One mile west of downtown, this 150-room hotel has an outdoor pool and free parking. Two people, $46 to $76. Address: 1800 West End Avenue, Nashville, TN 37203. Phone: 615-327-0922; 800-325-2525.

Econo Lodge—East: Ten miles east of downtown, this 70-room motel has an outdoor pool. Two people, $34 to $49. Address: 3445 Percy Priest Drive at I-40, Nashville, TN 37214. Phone: 615-889-8881.

Guest Quarters Suite Hotel: Six miles east of downtown, these 138 suites include a refrigerator with complimentary coffee, tea, and juices. Indoor and outdoor pools and airport shuttle service. Two people, $112 to $125. Address: 2424 Atrium Way, Nashville, TN 37210. Phone: 615-889-8889; 800-242-2900.

Hampton Inn—Vanderbilt: One mile west of downtown, this 171-room hotel has an outdoor pool and free parking. Complimentary continental breakfast and exercise facility. Two people, $53 to $60. Address: 1919 West End Avenue, Nashville, TN 37203. Phone: 615-329-1144; 800-426-7866.

Howard Johnson Lodge: Eight miles east of downtown, this 48-room hotel offers complimentary continental breakfast and an outdoor pool. Pets are allowed. Two people, $34 to $65. I-40 and Stewarts Ferry Pike, Nashville, TN 37214. Phone: 615-391-8074; 800-346-4974.

Quality Inn Hermitage: Ten miles east of downtown, this 65-room hotel offers nonsmoking rooms and rooms with whirlpool baths. Queen-sized beds and hair dryers in every room. Indoor and outdoor pools. Complimentary continental breakfast. Two people, $43 to $70. I-40 at Old

Hickory Blvd., Hermitage, TN 37076. Phone: 615-871-4545; 800-752-0773.

Super 8 Motel—Nashville Airport: Eight miles east of downtown, this 100-room motel has a shuttle service to the airport. Two people, $42 to $52. Address: 720 Royal Parkway, Nashville, TN 37214. Phone: 615-889-8887; 800-843-1991.

Bed & Breakfasts

There are some lovely Bed & Breakfast accommodations within twenty miles of Nashville. If you enjoy the personal touch of staying in the host's home and meeting your fellow guests at the complimentary breakfasts, this could be a pleasant change from motels or hotels.

Most Bed & Breakfast accommodations take credit cards, require advance reservations, do not accept pets, and may not accept children. Unless otherwise noted, they are not equipped to accommodate people with disabilities.

For a complete listing of area B & Bs, write:

Bed & Breakfast Hospitality—Tennessee
P.O. Box 110227
Nashville, TN 37222.
Phone: 615-331-5244; 800-458-2421
    outside Tennessee.

Here are some special places:

The Hancock House: Twenty miles northeast of downtown, this historic two-story log house has fifteen rooms to let, including two suites, two kitchenettes, and one room equipped to accommodate the disabled. There also is a separate cabin available. Most rooms have a private bath and fireplace. Full breakfast served. Jacuzzi, golf, swimming, and tennis available. Two people, $60 to $150. Address: 2144 Nashville Pike, Gallatin, TN 37066. Phone: 615-452-8431.

Lyric Springs Country Inn: Located in Franklin, eighteen miles south of downtown Nashville, this sprawling western cedar is home to Patsy Bruce, cowriter of "Mommas, Don't Let Your Babies Grow Up to Be Cowboys." Three rooms are furnished in antiques and music memorabilia. Order spa services, like a massage, manicure, or pedicure, when you make your reservations. Bring your horse—stable available, and ride the Natchez Trace Trails. Or play billiards in the Old West Saloon. Complimentary breakfast. Arrangements can be made for lunch and dinner when you reserve the room. Two people, $90. From downtown Nashville, take I-65 south to Tennessee 96. Go west 13.9 miles to Old Harding Road. Turn right on South Harpeth. Address: 7306 S. Harpeth Road, Franklin, TN 37064. Phone: 615-329-3385; 800-621-7824.

Monthaven: This mansion on the National Register of Historic Places is fifteen miles northeast of downtown in Hendersonville. The Greek Revival mansion, built in the mid-1800s, served as a field hospital for Union and Confederate troops during the Civil War. Filled with antiques and family treasures, Monthaven has three guest rooms with private baths. A log cabin beside the house also is available. Swimming, a fitness center, and tennis are available nearby. Breakfast is served in the elegant dining room. Rooms in the house, $75; the cabin, $85. Address: 1154 Main Street, Hendersonville, TN 37075. Phone: 615-824-6319.

Campgrounds

Fiddlers Inn Campground: This 122-site campground provides an outdoor pool, store, laundry, showers, playground, and shuttles to Opryland. Full-service site, $18. Address: 2404 Music Valley Drive, Nashville, TN 37214. Phone: 615-885-1440.

Holiday Nashville Travel Park: This 300-site park offers an outdoor pool, store, laundry, showers, playground, and shuttles to area attractions. Full-service site, $22. Address: 2572 Music Valley Drive, Nashville, TN 37214. Phone: 615-889-4225.

Two Rivers Campground: With 113 sites, enjoy an outdoor pool, showers, laundry, store, playground, and area shuttles. Full-service site, $21. Address: 2616 Music Valley Drive, Nashville, TN 37214. Phone: 615-883-8559.

Nashville KOA: With 460 sites, campers enjoy a pool, store, laundry, showers, shuttles to area attractions, playground, and live entertainment from April through October. Full-service sites, $16.75 to $29.75. Address: 2626 Music Valley Drive, Nashville, TN 37214. Phone: 615-889-0282; 800-833-6995.

IMPORTANT ADDRESSES & PHONE NUMBERS

Nashville Convention and Visitors Bureau
161 Fourth Avenue, North
Nashville, TN 37219
Phone: 615-259-4700.

★ Police, ambulance or fire emergencies: 911.
★ Tennessee Highway Patrol: 615-741-2060.

★ National Weather Service, Nashville: 615-244-9393.

State information:

Tennessee Tourism Development
P.O. Box 23170
Nashville, TN 37219
Phone: 615-741-2158.

HISTORY

Nashville didn't get its start from country music. This city on the Cumberland River was established in 1710 by French fur traders. In 1778 an Englishman visited the river bluffs and decided it would be a good place for a permanent settlement.

The following year, James Robertson and John Donelson established Fort Nashborough, named for General Francis Nash of North Carolina. A replica of the fort, located near its original site in downtown Nashville, is open to visitors.

After Tennessee became the sixteenth state in 1796, Andrew Jackson began his rise to prominence from his home in Nashville. After his term as the seventh president, Jackson retired to the Hermitage, and is buried there beside his wife Rachel, daughter of John Donelson.

Another Nashvillian, William Walker, also became a president—of Nicaragua—in 1856, in an attempt to unite the countries of Central America.

Nashville became the permanent state capital in 1843. The capitol building was designed by Philadelphia architect William Strickland, who also designed the steeple on Independence Hall. Strickland became so involved with the capitol building that he asked to be interred within its walls. His crypt is in the northeast section of the Capitol.

During the Civil War, Nashville became a location important to Federal troops because of its river location and the railroad link from Louisville to Nashville, Chattanooga, and Atlanta. For three years the city was occupied by Federal troops. The Battle of Nashville, in 1864, was the last aggressive action of the Confederate Army.

In the decades that followed, Nashville's printing industry grew. It also became an important merchandise distribution center. But education became the most significant boon for the growing city.

When John Donelson brought settlers down the Cumberland River to Nashville, classes for the children in the party were held on the decks of the flatboats. Shortly after the settlement was founded, Robertson acquired a land grant from North Carolina to establish the Davidson Academy, now the University of Nashville. And until the Civil War, the Nashville Female Academy was distinguished in its education of women.

In 1866, Fisk University was founded as one of the first private schools dedicated to the education of African-Americans. Vanderbilt University was founded in 1873. In 1876, Meharry Medical College, which has educated more black doctors than all other medical colleges, was established. There are now seventeen colleges and universities in Nashville.

It may be the city's long dedication to higher education that explains the reticence of some Nashvillians to embrace the development of country music's influence in the city. Although John Donelson's journal records that religious services, music, and dancing were part of the two-day celebration when the flatboats arrived at the bluffs, the country music industry is still viewed as a "poor cousin" by some city residents.

However, in 1991 the 10 million visitors to Music City USA added $1.6 billion in direct sales to the economy. Of the nine performing-arts facilities in town, six feature primarily country performances. And several of the city's major annual events revolve around country music, including the International Country Music Fan Fair, a June event sponsored by the Grand Ole Opry and the Country Music Association. The week-long festival features more than 35 hours of stage shows, along with photograph and autograph sessions with lots of country music stars.

And visitors can feel relatively safe in this city of a half-million people. Nashville boasts the eighth lowest crime rate in the United States for cities with populations of more than 250,000.

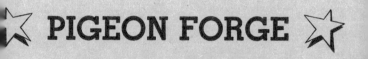

PIGEON FORGE

☆ For a spectacular shopping frenzy—with a taste of country music thrown in for relaxation—Pigeon Forge is *the* destination. This eastern Tennessee hamlet of 3000 people is home to Dollywood, a theme park co-owned by movie star and songstress Dolly Parton.

Pigeon Forge also is home to more than 200 outlet stores offering big discounts on all the brand-name stuff you've been waiting to buy.

And for year-round fun, try Pigeon Forge in November and December during the annual Winterfest celebration. For details, see the Pigeon Forge annual Calendar of Events.

It's all here—shoppers' paradise, country music shows, and all the good southern cooking you can pack away—at prices that don't raise the eyebrows or the line of credit. And at the outskirts of Pigeon Forge are misty mountains, the highest range east of the Mississippi.

Pigeon Forge lies at the gateway to Smoky Mountain National Park, with its headquarters and Visitors Center just south of Gatlinburg, five miles away. Last year, 8.6 million people visited the park. More than half of those visitors spent some time exploring "the strip"—a six-mile section of U.S. 441 that runs through Pigeon Forge.

The outlet malls are the biggest draw. Forty-two percent of the $379 million gross receipts from tourism last year came from Pigeon Forge's five outlet malls. More than 200 factory-direct bargain stores line the strip. Top-sellers include J. Crew, Nike, Geoffrey Beene, Fieldcrest Canon, and Liz Claiborne.

But that's not the end of the purchasing possibilities in Pigeon Forge. In area craft shops visitors can watch craftspeople weaving, quilting, and working pewter—old crafts performed by a new generation of craft makers.

If the kids aren't thrilled about shopping, don't worry. There are enough go-cart tracks, mini-golf courses, and water slides to keep youngsters and teens occupied for hours.

DON'T MISS!! One amazing attraction midway along the strip that children of all ages might enjoy is the FlyAway, a vertical wind tunnel, for a taste of sky-diving inside. Over the blast of DC-3 propellers, visitors can pay to soar to 21 feet off the ground inside a padded cage. If you don't feel like flying, it's fun to just watch, too.

The prime country music attraction in Pigeon Forge is Dollywood. The park is located one mile east of U.S. 441 on Dollywood Lane, at the south end of the strip. Parton, who was born in Sevier County, performs benefit concerts at the park opening weekend. Money raised from the concerts goes to the Dollywood Foundation to benefit education in Sevier County. Also, each weekend from the first weekend in May through the last weekend in October, the Celebrity Concert Series at Dollywood's Celebrity Theatre plays host to big-name country talent. Among those who have appeared are Vince Gill, Tanya Tucker, and the Statler Brothers.

For young people (of all ages), the ninety-acre park offers thrilling rides, including the Slidewinder, which leaves riders smiling—and drenched. For a drier, more relaxing ride, the Dollywood Express is a 110-ton coal-fired steam train that wends through the flower-filled park on a five-mile track.

Another bright spot in Dollywood is the antique hand-carved Dentzel carousel, nearly a century old. The magic sounds, reminiscent of romantic movies of the forties, come from a Gavioli pipe organ built in Paris. The carousel features 48 peaceful-looking animals, including lions, zebras, and ostriches.

After Dollywood and the outlets, save some energy for Pigeon Forge's country music shows. Five theaters on the strip plus the Mountain Music Amphitheater, at the north end of the strip, present evening variety shows that invite the audience to sing along, clap, or stomp a foot. Shows feature country, bluegrass, patriotic, and gospel music, along with production numbers including a fair amount of the traditional mountain clog dancing—an energetic ritual that resembles tap dancing without taps.

DON'T MISS!! Try an evening at the Dixie Stampede, near the turnoff to Dollywood at the south end of the strip. It's an 80,000-square-foot complex where you can get a four-course meal in a horse arena—complete with performing equestrians and a competition re-creating the rivalry between North and South. The show features runaway horse-drawn wagons and a thoroughbred pig race. Last year, visitors to the Dixie Stampede consumed more than 400,000 roast chickens.

Sleeping is easy in this town that goes to bed by 11 P.M. There are 65 motels and hotels and 13 campgrounds.

BUDGET ALERT!! Beware of the seasonal shift in prices that can raise a $25-a-night motel off-season from January through April, to $90 a night from May through October. Prices during the special Christmas season events in November and December are mid-range.

Eating out is not a wallet buster in Pigeon Forge. Billed as a "family fun destination," county liquor laws prohibit alcoholic beverages. That keeps the swankier, higher-priced restaurants out. The focus here is all-you-can-eat buffets, plenty of low-cost alternatives for the toddlers, and chicken fried steak everywhere. For a glass of wine with dinner, head south five miles to Gatlinburg.

Now let's get down to the serious stuff you need to know before you arrive in Pigeon Forge.

GETTING THERE

Pigeon Forge is 198 miles from Nashville, 230 miles from Atlanta, 31 miles southeast of Knoxville, five miles north of Gatlinburg. By car, from Interstate 40, which passes through Knoxville, take U.S. 441 south. Pigeon Forge lies on the edge of the mountains, but the terrain is flat.

The closest major airport is Knoxville, served by several major airlines, including American, Northwest, and United. There are several major rental car agencies at the Knoxville airport. Greyhound Bus Lines also provides service to

Pigeon Forge from its hub in Knoxville. For information on bus service, call 1-800-528-0447.

GETTING AROUND

Most of the attractions in Pigeon Forge are located on either side of a six-lane section of U.S. 441, known as "the strip" and called the Parkway. The primary exception is Dollywood, located one mile east of the strip on Dollywood Lane.

TIP! The strip, with three lanes of traffic in either direction, and divided by a landscaped median, can be difficult to cross on foot because the traffic signals are spaced about a mile apart. Pedestrians have to rely on the good graces of motorists to stop.

Likewise, you should be particularly cautious and patient when turning across the Parkway to change directions. In 1991 more than 96,000 cars traveled the Parkway.

An alternative is to leave your car at your strip motel and take the *Fun Time Trolley*. The San Francisco–style open-air trolleys operate from April through December, 8 A.M. to midnight. The trolleys make stops every block or on request. From any point, you won't have to wait more than twenty to thirty minutes for the next trolley to pass.

TIP! To get from one end of the strip to an attraction at the other end could take about an hour, so allow plenty of time if you're going by trolley. They are handicapped-accessible. Fare is 25 cents per ride. Tokens can be purchased for a discount (ten for $2, twenty for $3.50) at the Department of Tourism Welcome Center toward the north end of the strip, at 1159 Parkway. For more information, call the Fun Time Trolley office, 615-453-6444.

Weather: Summer temperatures average 80 degrees, but a hot day in summer could reach the low nineties. Summer nights near the mountains cool down comfortably. Some may even want a sweater or light jacket on summer evenings by the Little Pigeon River.

During the winter it's not unusual for snow to cap the nearby mountaintops, leaving the Pigeon Forge valley sunny and mild. Winter daytime temperatures average in the mid-forties to mid-fifties. Nights can get below freezing.

Dress: Casual is the key word here. Anything's in style in Pigeon Forge, as long as it's comfortable. No place requires a jacket or tie.

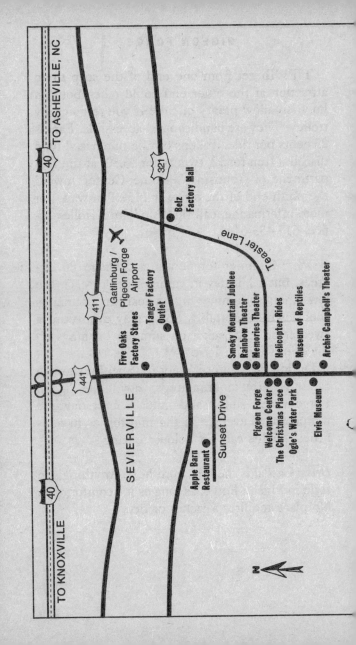

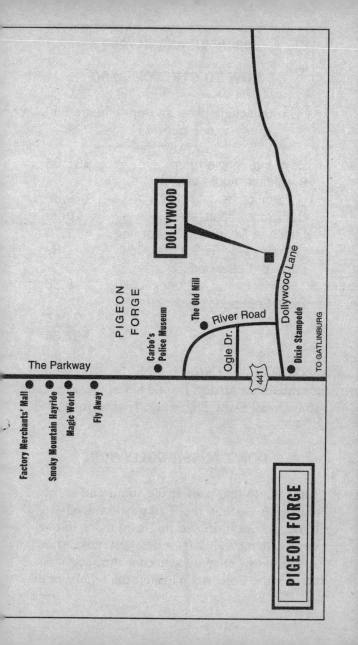

PIGEON FORGE

Factory Merchants' Mall
Smoky Mountain Hayride
Magic World
Fly Away

The Parkway

PIGEON FORGE

Carbo's
Police Museum

The Old Mill

River Road

Ogle Dr.

441

Dixie Stampede

Dollywood Lane

TO GATLINBURG

DOLLYWOOD

HOW TO STRETCH $100

(Costs include taxes and tips and are for
one person.)

Days Inn, single room	$37.66
Breakfast, Apple Valley Farmhouse	9.86
Dollywood, adult admission	19.99
Lunch at Dollywood: hot dog	1.79
small Coke	.89
Later at Dollywood . . . funnel cake	3.30
Dixie Stampede, includes dinner	24.15
	$97.64

POSSIBLE SPLURGE!! With the $100 allotted
for the following day, I could have purchased the
16-inch-tall Dolly Doll at Dollywood for $69.95.

DON'T MISS!! DOLLYWOOD

This ninety-acre park at the south end of town,
one mile east of the Parkway on Dollywood
Lane, is a beautiful setting to wander through,
even without the crafts, rides, and music shows.

The music shows, except for the special concerts in the Celebrity Theater, run hourly, or ev-

ery two hours, throughout the day. The shows are fun, a good chance to rest your tired feet.

Dollywood opened in 1961 as Rebel Railroad. The small park featured the steam train, a general store, blacksmith shop, and a saloon. In 1970 the park was purchased by the Cleveland Browns football team and was renamed Goldrush Junction. The Browns added a campground, log cabins, a wood shop, barn, grist mill, and several children's rides.

In 1976, Herschend Enterprises, owners of Silver Dollar City in Branson, Missouri, purchased the park. They operated it for one season under the Goldrush name, then changed it to Silver Dollar City, Tennessee, in 1976.

By May 1986, when the Herschends joined forces with Dolly Parton and renamed the park, it had doubled in size and expanded to become a full-fledged theme park.

Dollywood can be done in a day, unless there's a special event at the park that takes up your attention. Here's what to watch for:

Music Shows

Celebrity Theater: The Showcase of Stars presents big-name entertainers like Ricky Skaggs, Tanya Tucker, Vince Gill, Charlie Daniels, Conway Twitty, and Roy Clark. Concerts are held in the

1739-seat indoor amphitheater inside the park, weekends at 2 and 7 P.M., from the first weekend in May through the last weekend in October. In July there are concerts twice daily, at 2 and 7 P.M.

On opening weekend, April 24 and 25, Dolly Parton performs benefit concerts twice daily at 2 and 7 P.M. Funds raised go to help Sevier County schools. Prices for the fund-raiser range from $500, for a front-row seat, to $35.

To get the annual schedule, or make reservations, call 615-428-9620 or 615-428-9630.

Admission ranges from $8.99 to $11.99, depending on the artist and the date. The 2 P.M. show requires park admission. A ticket for the 7 P.M. show admits you to the concert only.

Dolly's Mountain Music: Tunes that recall the musical influences of Dolly's youth.

Dollywood Jamboree: A popular mixture of pop, country, oldies, and comedy for all ages.

The James Rogers Show: A one-man show with an amazing variety.

The Kingdom Heirs: Award-winning gospel music.

The Randy Parton Show: Dolly's brother sings contemporary country favorites mixed with some of Randy's originals.

The Showstreet Palace: "Fire on the Mountain" is presented every two hours in this new 1000-seat theater. It's a song and dance story of Indians and settlers, with some pyrotechnic special effects for the grand finale.

Wings of America: Multimedia show that is entertaining and educational about birds of prey, from eagles to owls.

Special Sights in Dollywood

DON'T MISS!! *Eagle Mountain Sanctuary:* This 1.5-million-cubic-foot fenced area is home to the largest flock of "nonreleasable" bald eagles in America. These are birds who've been wounded, raised in captivity, or for some reason are unable to exist in the wild. It's stunning to see these big beauties so close.

All the birds here are under the care of the National Foundation to Protect America's Eagles. They are authorized by the U.S. Fish and Wildlife Service and the Tennessee Wildlife Resource Agency to keep birds for rehabilitation, breeding, exhibition, and education.

Dentzel Carousel: A hand-carved, 100-year-old merry-go-round with 48 animals from horses to ostriches. This one sounds like a carousel should!

The Dolly Parton Story: This museum with hundreds of mementos tells Dolly's "rags to riches" story.

The Dollywood Express: Take the five-mile ride on this 100-ton coal-fired steam engine. It's relaxing and gives a good overview of the park.

Friendship Gardens: More than 30,000 flowering plants. Stroll, or sit on a bench.

Imagination Station: Let the kiddies learn a thing or two with Construction Junction's giant building blocks. At Creativity Corner, helpers let kids produce a craft all their own. In the Bubble Works, wraparound bubble tubes and bubble walls are fun to see.

Crafts are the backbone of Dollywood. In addition to purchasing the wares, you can see craftspeople at work, demonstrating old and new skills in making baskets, brooms, candles, dulcimers, soap, pottery, quilts, sand casts, and wagons. Watch the blacksmith pound out the glowing iron, or see glass blowers in their goggles making intricate ships.

The fall craft festival adds even more fascinating demonstrations and goodies to purchase.

DON'T MISS!! *Dolly's Dressing Room.* This shop features glitzy and glamorous clothing like the stars might wear. TIP! Check the rear of shops.

It's where many have the bargains, and even theme park shops have sales.

Rides

Beware! While most are fairly tame, some will get you drenched. Signs warn about what to expect. Some rides have minimum height requirements.

* Smoky Mountain Rampage: A twisting adventure through whitewater rapids.
* Mountain Slidewinder: This slip-sliding ride on a water toboggan makes a big splash.
* Blazing Fury: Ride through a burning town that's filled with animated surprises. Know what puts out a fire? Water!
* Flooded Mine: Journey by boat through a flooded mine.
* Thunder Express: Your basic roller coaster, but twisting among the treetops.
* Fun Country: Lots of rides for the tykes, including airplanes and semi trucks to drive.

Dining

A breakfast buffet is served beginning an hour before the park opens at Aunt Granny's Restaurant. Served until 10:30 A.M. for $4.99; ages 11 and under, $2.99.

BUDGET ALERT!! Summer Dinner Specials from Memorial Day to Labor Day, from 4 P.M. to closing time. Five of the park's restaurants offer different menus with dinners for $5.95, including Miss Lillian's Chicken House, Hickory House Bar-B-Q, Aunt Granny's Restaurant, and the Whistlestop Steakhouse.

Lots to choose from, including honey-stung chicken at Miss Lillian's Chicken House. Plate lunch includes slaw, beans, roll, and cobbler for $5.99. Or lunch on sausage, red beans, and rice at Granny Ogle's Ham 'n Beans.

BUDGET ALERT!! Unless you can't live without a bubbly drink with your meal, ask for a glass of water. Cokes at Dollywood range from $.89 to $1.29. For a large family, it adds up.

Calendar of Events, 1993

May 7–31: The American Quilt Showcase. Handmade quilts and quilters from all over. Featured is the Royal Stars of the States, a fifty-quilt collection representing every state's official star.

October 1–30: The National Crafts Festival. The Smokies' oldest and largest harvest festival brings craftmakers from across the country. Cooking crafts also are part of the fun. Try hoecakes, handmade pretzels, and mountain chili pies.

November 12–December 30: Smoky Mountain Christmas. More than a million lights brighten the park during this celebration. The train is decked in lights and takes visitors on a fantasy journey to Santa's Smoky Mountain Headquarters. Christmas shows fill the theaters, and handbell choirs and strolling carolers fill the streets.

Here's some details to get you going:

For 1993, the park opens April 24 and 25 from 9 A.M. to 9 P.M.; April 30, 10 A.M. to 6 P.M.

In May it's open daily except Thursdays, from 10 A.M. to 6 P.M.; 9 A.M. to 9 P.M. Saturdays; and 10 A.M. to 7 P.M. Sundays.

June, July, and August the park is open daily from 9 A.M. to 9 P.M.

In September the park closes on Wednesdays and Thursdays. Park hours are 10 A.M. to 6 P.M. except Saturdays, when it is open 9 A.M. to 7 P.M.

In October it's closed on Thursday. Hours are 10 A.M. to 6 P.M.; Saturdays, 9 A.M. to 7 P.M.

In November the park is closed from November 1 through 11. It reopens November 12 and is open Fridays, Saturdays, and Sundays only through November 28. Hours have not been set.

In December it's open Fridays, Saturdays, and Sundays from December 3 through 19. It's also open December 22, 23, and 26 through 30. Hours have not been set.

Admission:
April 25 through November 1:

> 1-day adult ticket (ages 12 and up) $19.99
> 1-day child ticket (ages 4 through 11) $13.99
> 1-day senior ticket (60 and up) $16.99

Christmas season November 13 through January 3:

> 1-day adult ticket $12.99
> 1-day child ticket $7.99

Come after 3 P.M. and the next day's admission is free. Strollers, wheelchairs and electric carts are available to rent.

For further information, if you're inside east Tennessee, call: 615-428-9488; outside east Tennessee, 1-800-DOLLYWOOD.

COUNTRY MUSIC SHOWS

Pigeon Forge music shows have a distinct down-home flavor. Two of them, Archie Campbell's Hee Haw Theater and the Smoky Mountain Jubilee, got their start in Branson before finding a home in Tennessee.

The theaters are cozy, so you won't need binoculars to see the performers. There are plenty of spangled costumes, singing, dancing and hillbilly comedy.

The shows are distinctly geared for families: no one will be offended, and the children are welcome. Some shows are free to children under age 12. After the show, most of the performers stay to sign autographs and greet their fans.

Reservations are a good idea. Call ahead and avoid a wait in line or a sold-out show. Traditionally, the shows have offered evening-only performances. But more are adding an afternoon matinee and staying open into December's Winterfest.

The Archie Campbell Theater presents Phil Campbell's "Hee Haw" Show: Country comedy with old and new country songs in this 250-seat theater. Add a helping of bluegrass and gospel too. The show features Phil Campbell of "Hee Haw" fame and his band, Tennessee. Archie Campbell also operated the Hee Haw Theater in Branson from 1981 until it closed in 1983. Open April 24 through October. Shows nightly at 8:30 P.M. Admission: $9; children under 12, $6. Address: 918 Parkway. Phone: 615-428-3218.

Bonnie Lou and Buster's Smoky Mountain Hayride Show: Featuring Little Roy Wiggins, who appeared on the Grand Ole Opry and the "Eddie Arnold Show." The show in this 850-seat theater includes the Smoky Mountain Sweetheart Cloggers, banjo-pickin' country tunes, and comedy by the Briar Thicket Hillbillies. Nightly at 8:30 P.M. Admission: $7.50; children under 12 free. Open mid-April through November. Address: 3870 Parkway. Phone: 615-453-9590; 615-428-0196.

DON'T MISS!! *The Dixie Stampede:* Enjoy a four-course meal including a whole roasted chicken, dessert, and beverages in a 1000-seat arena. While you eat, an array of thirty horses and riders pays tribute to the Civil War. The "conflict" is decided by barrel races, wagon sprints, even a pig race. Audience participation, by cheering and clapping, is invited. Adults, $21.95; children ages 4–12, $12.95. Closed January and February. Open weekends March, April, November, and December with shows at 6:30 P.M. May through October open daily with shows at 6:30 and 8:30 P.M. Address: 3849 Parkway, one block south of Dollywood Lane. Phone: 615-453-4400; 1-800-356-1676.

Memories Theatre: Eddie Miles presents a "Salute to Elvis" nightly at 8:30 P.M. Hear all your favorite Elvis songs from a look-alike, sound-alike. After the show, he stays to sign autographs. The show also features music from the fifties and sixties, plus comedy. Open daily March through September. October through mid-December, open Tuesday through Saturday. Admission: $10; ages 5 through 10, $4; under 5, free. Address: 2141 Parkway. Phone: 615-428-7852.

Music Mountain Amphitheater: This 3500-seat outdoor amphitheater features nightly country music concerts from Memorial Day through Labor Day, with weekend-only concerts beginning in mid-June. Ticket prices range from $10 to $15. Address: 2303 Parkway. For current scheduling information, call 615-428-3441.

Rainbow Music Theatre: A variety show starring Dick Dale, 32-year veteran of "The Lawrence Welk Show," and Ava Barber, who performed with Welk for ten years. Backed by a five-piece band, the show in this 270-seat theater also features the Fiddlin' Wallace Sisters. Open May through October with shows Monday through Saturday at 8:15 P.M., matinees at 2 P.M. Weekend shows through November. Special Winterfest performances. Admission: $9.50; children 12 and under free. Address: 1100 Parkway. Phone: 615-428-5600.

Smoky Mountain Jubilee: This show originated in Branson in 1977. Five years later, owners Elmer and Faunda Dreyer relocated in Pigeon Forge. A cast of seventeen provides country, bluegrass, gospel, flag-waving, and clogging nightly at 8:30 P.M. in this 900-seat theater. Closed January and February. Weekends only November, December, March, and April. Monday through Saturday from Labor Day through Memorial Day. Admission: $9.50; children under 12, $4. Address: 2115 Parkway. Phone: 615-428-1836.

BREAKING INTO THE PIGEON FORGE MUSIC SCENE

From June 25 through July 1 check out the Rising Star Talent Competition at the Grand Hotel. The competitors have been selected through regional competitions in nineteen cities. They compete in vocal, dance, group, and several other categories. Winners of the national finals in Pigeon Forge, which may feature as many as 5000 competitors during the week-long show, have been hired at Dollywood and the Dixie Stampede. National talent scouts also are invited. There is a fee for entering the competition. Groups, for example, pay $12 per member. To receive more information about the regional competitions, write Rising Star Talent Productions, P.O. Box 30925, Gahanna, Ohio 43230. Or call 614-478-4333.

There is also the 10th Annual Talent Show at the Smoky Mountain Jubilee Theater. The first forty applicants get to show their talents. Most are single or group vocalists, but each year there are some instrumentalists, dancers, and comedians, says theater owner Elmer Dreyer. Remember, this is good, clean, family entertainment. For an application, write Smoky Mountain Jubilee, P.O. Box 1316, Pigeon Forge, TN 37863. Phone: 615-428-1836.

SHOPPING

Put on your most comfortable shoes and grab your checkbook. Fortunately, Citizens National Bank, First National Bank, and Sevier County Bank serve Cirrus, Most, Money Belt, and Plus System bank cards.

A shopping marathon can easily run three days in Pigeon Forge. Lots of gift and craft shops dot the Parkway, in addition to the factory outlet malls. Here's a roundup of some of the most unusual.

Cat House and Critter Cottage: Hundreds of gift items, all featuring cats. Handmade cloth cat dolls designed and sewn by owner Cheryl Anderson, on her 1901 treadle sewing machine. Open daily 10 A.M. to 7 P.M. Winter hours, 10 A.M. to 5 P.M. Address: 3327 Old Mill Street. Phone: 615-428-6133.

DON'T MISS!! *The Christmas Place:* It's always the season to be jolly in this Bavarian-style shop that features more than 100 decorated trees. The Small World Transportation Company offers a big selection of trains and accessories of all shapes and sizes. Collectible lines for sale including Llardro, David Winter Cottages, Hummel and Swarovski Crystal. Open daily 9 A.M. to 10:30 P.M. January through March, 9 A.M. to 6 P.M. On the Parkway in Bell Tower Square. 615-453-0415.

Crafts for Less: Everything to do-it-yourself, from quilting to cake decorating supplies. Open daily 9 A.M. to 7 P.M. Address: 3121 Parkway. Phone: 615-453-6232.

Jim Gray Gallery: Paintings, prints, sculpture, and pottery created by nationally-renowned artist Jim Gray. Open daily 9 A.M. to 4 P.M., on River Road across from the Old Mill. Phone: 615-428-2202.

Old Mill Craft Village: Located behind the Old Mill on Middle Creek Road, these 25 specialty shops add variety to the town's wares. Selections include the Highlands British Shoppe, Helix Pewter, the Pigeon Forge Craft Center, and Stella Mae's Doll Shoppe. A picnic grounds is available next to the Little Pigeon River, and visitors can feed the ducks.

Old Time Pottery: No fancy showroom, but bargain prices on pottery and giftware. Next to Belz Mall. Open daily 9 A.M. to 6 P.M. Phone: 615-453-6882.

Ole Smoky General Store: Built with fixtures, shelves, and counters from the Ransley Burge Mallory General Store built in 1893 in Clyo, Georgia. The store sells antique goods from cherry pitters to tin ware. Leather tack and buggy accessories, garden seeds, handmade baskets, jellies, herbs, and spices give the feel of a return to earlier times. Closed February. Open daily 9 A.M. to 9 P.M. Address: 2713 Parkway. Phone: 615-453-5330.

Pigeon Forge Pottery: In 1937, potter Douglas Ferguson visited the Old Mill and found the layered mud nests made by the mud dauber wasp. That led him to discover the type of clay a potter needs. Ferguson still uses the native clay to create a range of pottery and giftware in his shop on Middle Creek Road in the Old Mill Craft Village. Open daily 8 A.M. to 5 P.M. Phone 615-453-3704.

Randall Ogle Gallery: Paintings, limited edition prints, and miniatures by Randall Ogle. Known internationally, Ogle is the descendant of the area's earliest settlers. Open year-round, except Sundays, 10:30 A.M. to 4 P.M. Next to the Old Mill. Phone: 615-428-2839.

Outlet Malls

Hope you're not tired. The fun is just beginning. There are more than 200 factory outlet stores offering discounts of up to 75 percent every day.

Belz Factory Outlet Mall: Sixty stores, including Bon Worth, Converse, DonnKenny, Duckhead, Gitano, Jonathan Logan, Jordache, Maidenform, Royal Doulton, and Van Heusen. The *Outlet Annex* next door houses another 24 shops, including Bugle Boy, Westpoint Pepperell, Capezio, Members Only, and Nike.

Open daily. April through December: Monday through Saturday, 10 A.M. to 9 P.M.; Sunday, 10 A.M. to 6 P.M. January through March: Thursday through Friday, 10 A.M. to 6 P.M.; weekends, 10

A.M. to 9 P.M. Just east of the Parkway at 2655 Teaster Lane. Phone: 615-453-3503.

Factory Merchants Mall: Forty-six outlets, including American Tourister, Arrow Shirts, Black & Decker, Boston Traders, Buxton, Geoffrey Beene, Izod/Gant, Magnavox, and Rawlings Sporting Goods.

Open daily. January and February, Sunday through Thursday, 10 A.M. to 6 P.M.; Friday and Saturday, 10 A.M. to 9 P.M. March through December, Monday through Saturday, 9 A.M. to 9 P.M.; Sunday 9 A.M. to 6 P.M. Midway along the Parkway, under the red roof. Phone: 615-428-2828.

Five Oaks Factory Outlet: Twenty stores, including Woolrich, Brooks Brothers, Lenox China, Guess? Jeans, Dan River, and Reed & Barton. Open daily. Monday through Saturday, 9 A.M. to 9 P.M.; Sunday, 9 A.M. to 6 P.M. On the Parkway, just north of Pigeon Forge. Phone: 615-453-8401.

Tanger Factory Outlet Center: Twenty-five shops beneath the green-roofed mall, including Ann Klein, Barbizon Lingerie, Dansk, Eddie Bauer, J. Crew, Liz Claiborne, London Fog, and Reebok. Open daily. January through March: Sunday through Thursday, 10 A.M. to 6 P.M., Friday and Saturday, 10 A.M. to 9 P.M. April through

December, Monday through Saturday, 9 A.M. to 9 P.M.; Sunday, 9 A.M. to 6 P.M. Just east of the Parkway on Davis Road. Phone: 615-428-7001; 800-727-6885.

Z-Buda Outlet Mall: Thirty stores, including Bon Worth, Bumbershoot Books, Formfit Intimates, Country Cabin Crafts, Manhattan, and S. Mullins Leathergoods. Open daily. Monday through Saturday, 9 A.M. to 9 P.M.; Sunday, 9 A.M. to 6 P.M. Midway along the Parkway, next to Factory Merchants Mall.

OTHER ATTRACTIONS

If you want a day off from shopping, there are lots of other amusements on the Parkway. In addition to these listings, there are go-cart tracks, water slides, and arcades aplenty.

Here are some of the more memorable attractions:

Carbo's Smoky Mountain Police Museum: A private collection of police memorabilia from around the world. Weapons, uniforms, and a drug paraphernalia exhibit. The highlight is a collection of artifacts belonging to Buford Pusser, immortalized in the 1973 movie *Walking Tall.* The display includes the 1974 Corvette in which he mysteriously died. Open weekends in April. May through October, open daily 10 A.M. to 5 P.M. Closed on Thursday in May, September, and October. Admission: $5; children 10 and under, $3. Address: 3311 Parkway. 615-453-1358.

Elvis Presley Museum: Elvis memorabilia, including a limousine used by Elvis, as well as clothing, guns, and jewelry owned by The King. All items are guaranteed by the owners to be authentic. Open year round. Daily in summer from 9 A.M. to 9 P.M. Winter hours: 10 A.M. to 6 P.M. Admission: $4.99; children 6 to 10, $2.99. Address: 1019 Parkway. Phone: 615-453-6499.

DON'T MISS!! *FlyAway Indoor Skydiving:* For the past ten years, visitors have been able to get a feel for skydiving inside a vertical wind tunnel. Instructors help fliers afloat and maneuver within the padded chamber. Powered by a propeller from a DC-3 beneath a mesh screen on the chamber's floor, winds reach 120 mph in the 21-foot-high chamber. Instruction for first-time fliers takes an hour. Minimum weight for fliers is 40 pounds, maximum is 230. Closed in December. Open weekends only, January through March. Adults, $12.95; under 12, $11.95. Address: 3106 Parkway. Phone: 615-453-7777.

Guinness World Records Exhibition Center: Ten galleries of displays and information on the fastest

. . . longest . . . tallest . . . Included is a display of Beatles memorabilia. Open daily 9 A.M. to 10 P.M. Address: 631 Parkway. Phone: 615-436-9100.

Magic World Kids Park: Rides and games for kids of all ages. A sixty-foot-tall Ferris wheel overlooks the Tilt-A-Whirl and the Dragon Coaster rides. Open daily 10 A.M. to 5 P.M. May through September. Weekends in April and November. Admission: $11.95; children under two free. Go-carts cost $1 extra. Address: 3034 Parkway. Phone: 615-453-7941.

Museum of Reptiles: Live exhibits of cobras, rattlesnakes, and other creatures. The museum's motto is: "Awareness, conservation, and ecology through education." Open daily 10 A.M. to 10 P.M., March through September; Friday, Saturday, and Sunday, October through December. Admission $4; $2.50 age 10 and under. Across the Parkway from the Red Roof Factory Outlet on the north end of the Parkway. Phone: 615-428-4427.

Ogle's Water Park: With eight slides, there's a thrill level for everyone. For immersion therapy, there's a wave pool and the Lil' Tyke Lagoon. For those afraid of water, the park includes a miniature golf course. Also has dressing rooms and lockers. Open daily at 10 A.M. June through

August. Open weekends at 11 A.M. in May. Address: 2530 Parkway. Phone: 615-453-8741.

DON'T MISS!! *The Old Mill:* History combines with postcard-picturesque at this working mill on the banks of the Little Pigeon River. Grinding is done on a two-ton stone, installed when the mill was built in 1830, powered by a 24-foot water wheel.

The Mill is supported on 14-inch-square yellow poplar logs forty feet long, resting on pillars built of river rock. The interior is hand-hewn hemlock and oak held together with hickory pegs.

The iron forge, for which the town was named, sat beside the mill until it was dismantled in 1885. In the gift shop you can buy fresh-ground barley and buckwheat flour, cornmeal, and other grain flours. The coffee shop serves whole wheat biscuits with country ham. Open daily 8:30 A.M. to 6 P.M. One block east of the Parkway on River Road at the south end of the Parkway.

Smoky Mountain River Run: Tubing on the Little Pigeon River can be cool in the summer heat. The three-mile trip takes about two hours. Sneakers and a bathing suit are recommended attire. Adults, $10; children under 12, $8. Open daily June through September. Price includes transportation back to the put-in point. Address: 315 North River Road. Phone: 615-428-4403.

Smoky Mountain Scenic Flights: For an overview, hop a single-engine plane for a variety of flights over the area. The Sampler Tour lasts twenty to thirty minutes and flies over Pigeon Forge, Dollywood, and Gatlinburg. Cost: adults, $35; children, $25. To fly over the mountains for a view of Mt. Mitchell, the highest point in the eastern U.S., take the On Top of Old Smoky flight for fifty minutes. Adults, $50; children, $35. Flights leave hourly from Gatlinburg–Pigeon Forge Airport, about two miles east of U.S. 441 on U.S. 411. Shuttle service to the airport is available from many area motels. Phone: 615-428-2750.

In the Area: The Great Smoky Mountains National Park: This half-million acre wildlands sanctuary protects the largest virgin forest remaining in the eastern United States, unspoiled and looking much like the woods the first settlers discovered.

Restored log cabins and barns remind modern-day travelers of those who came before, when these mountains were a wilderness.

While the park has been tamed since then, it's still home to many species of wild animals, including deer, wild turkeys, and bears.

SAFETY ALERT!! This may sound like an unnecessary warning, but: if, while driving through the park, you see a bear, stay in your car and roll up the windows. FEEDING THE WILDLIFE IS AGAINST PARK REGULA-TIONS. The park has more than 900 miles of hiking trails, including self-guiding nature trails for short hikes.

From park headquarters, four miles south of Gatlinburg, at Sugarlands Visitor Center, take a one-mile introductory hike to become familiar with the human and natural history of the park.

Or you can head out from Sugarlands on a thirteen-mile hike past beautiful Rainbow Falls. Fishing is permitted year-round in open park waters, with a Tennessee or North Carolina fishing license.

For more information, contact the Smoky Mountain Visitors Bureau: 1004 Tuckaleechee Pk., Maryville, TN 37801. Phone: 615-984-6200; 800-251-9100 (outside Tennessee).

Gatlinburg: A drive into Gatlinburg, five miles south of Pigeon Forge on U.S. 441, is worth the trip. This is a quaint-looking town with the main street fashioned after a European village. Lots of fun shops and eateries line the five-mile strip.

A popular venue in Gatlinburg is the *Passion Play*. The musical play depicts Christ's death and resurrection. Before or after, visit the *Little Jerusalem Market Place* for Christian crafts. Open April thorough September, with shows Mondays through Saturdays at 8:30 P.M. Admission: $9.95; children, 5 to 12, $4.95. Located on Airport Road, just off U.S. 441. Phone: 615-430-3777.

For more information, write the Gatlinburg Chamber of Commerce, 520 Parkway, Gatlinburg, TN 37738. Or call, 615-436-4178; 800-822-1998.

Old Smoky Outfitters: These experienced folks can provide everything you need for a personally-guided fishing trip. Excursions are available for both experts and those new at fishing. Overnight, full, or half-day trips are available. A half-day guided trout fishing trip with a group costs $30 per person and includes rod, reel, bait, and box lunch. A half-day float trip with a guide on the Little Pigeon River, including lunch: $125 per person. Address: 511 Parkway. Phone: 615-430-1936.

Guided Tours:

Mountain Tours: A variety of tours, including a six-hour trip that meanders past the childhood home of Dolly Parton. From mid-June to late August, travel six hours to the Cherokee Indian Drama, where a cast of 130 recounts the tribe's history. Motel pickups. Cost: Adults, $26; children ages 4 through 11, $20. Phone: 615-453-0864.

Smoky Mountain Tours: Pickups for these bus tours are made at many area motels. They offer seven tour packages, including a 1½-hour tour to Newfound Gap mountaintop. Departs daily at 10 A.M. and 12:45 P.M. Cost: Adults, $12; children under 12, $7. If you have time, you might try the Las Vegas in the Smokies Tour. A six-hour trip takes you onto the Cherokee Indian Reservation, where slot machines are legal. Departs daily except Sundays at 5:30 P.M. Adults only, $15. Phone: 615-436-3471; 1-800-962-0448.

DINING

Dining in Pigeon Forge is easy on the pocketbook, with lots of family-style buffets in the $6.95 to $9.95 range.

For fancier, special-occasion meals, drive the five miles south to Gatlinburg, where liquor is served in most restaurants.

Restaurants included here take major credit cards, are handicapped-accessible, and are open year-round unless otherwise noted. TIP! Prices quoted for meals here are for one person.

The food is classic southern country, with chicken fried steak, ham and red-eye gravy, and corn bread prominent on most menus. For quickies, the normal array of fast-food chains is available on the Parkway, including McDonald's, Pizza Hut, and Taco Bell.

DON'T MISS!! *Applewood Farmhouse Restaurant:* Every meal begins with an Applewood julep (cider blended with other juices), apple fritters, and apple butter.

Breakfast prices range from $4.75 to $8.75 for choices that include eggs, biscuits, country ham, and red-eye gravy. Dinners start at $9.25 for the Orchard Fruit Plate to $15.95 for rib-eye steak.

Choose from several cozy rooms, each with a different decor, in the charming old farmhouse, built in 1921. After the meal, stroll through apple orchards to the cider mill, where cider is pressed from late August through mid-winter.

Don't miss the candy kitchen, where stick candy and jawbreakers are made in antique copper kettles, the old-fashioned way.

In the Apple Barn General Store, you can buy apples in season, and cleverly crafted gifts with an apple theme all year.

Open Thursday through Sunday, 8 A.M. to 9 P.M.; Fridays and Saturdays to 10 P.M. Located at the north end of the Parkway; turn west on Apple Valley Road. Phone: 615-428-1222.

Bennett's Pit Bar-B-Que: A varied menu includes a breakfast and fruit bar for $4.99, salads and sandwiches. A favorite is the jumbo baby-back rib rack, smoked over hickory logs for fourteen hours, for $15.99. Open year-round from Sundays through Thursdays, 8 A.M. to 10 P.M.; Fridays and Saturdays, 7 A.M. to 11 P.M. Address: 2910 Parkway. Phone: 615-429-2200.

Calabash Seafood: Although steaks and chicken are on the menu, the favorite is the all-you-can-eat seafood buffet, served daily for $14.95. Menu items include perch, catfish, shrimp, oysters, clams, crabs—and lobster tail for $21.95. Desserts include a devilish mudslide pie. Open daily 8 A.M. to 9 P.M. Closed January and February. Address: 421 Parkway. Phone: 615-428-3225.

Country Pickens Family Restaurant: An array of all-American food from beefburgers for $3.35 to pork chops for $6.85. Try a bacon and egg sandwich for lunch for $2.95. You can get slaw on the sandwich for an extra fifty cents if you ask. Open daily 7 A.M. to 10 P.M., with breakfast served until noon. At the Americana Inn, 2825 Parkway. Phone: 615-428-1972.

BUDGET ALERT!! *Duff's Smorgasbord:* This 300-seat restaurant is in the fourteenth year of serving family-style buffets featuring six kinds of meat, vegetables, salads, rolls, and dessert for $6.99. Good, basic food and pleasant atmosphere for a budget price. Open daily from 8 A.M. to 9 P.M. Address: 3985 Parkway. Phone: 615-453-6443.

Farmer's Daughter: Serving country breakfasts and lunch daily from 7 A.M. to 1 P.M. "Made from scratch" buttermilk biscuits are the specialty. Closed January through March. Address: 3509 Parkway. Phone: 615-453-6485.

Highlands British Shoppe: This departure features traditional English treats like meat pies for $2.75, bangers and mash (sausages and potatoes mashed with turnips) for $3.95. Try afternoon tea with scones for $1.20. The gift shop features wares from the British Isles. Open Monday through Saturday, 10 A.M. to 5:30 P.M.; Sundays 10 A.M. to 5 P.M. Two blocks east of the Parkway on Middle Creek Road in the Old Mill Craft Village. Phone: 615-428-2987.

DON'T MISS!! *Log Cabin Pancake House:* This homey dining room features more than three dozen varieties of pancakes and waffles, including chocolate chip pancakes and bacon waffles. Serving breakfast anytime, the restaurant also offers an all-you-can-eat buffet beginning at 4:30 P.M. Address: 4235 Parkway. Open daily 7 A.M. to 9:30 P.M.; November through March, 7 A.M. to 2 P.M. Phone: 615-453-5748.

Maples: Open daily 7 A.M. to 10 P.M. Breakfast buffet and fruit bar, $3.95. Evening buffet served Thursday through Saturday from 4:30

P.M., $8.95. Address: 4025 Parkway, in the Ramada Inn.

Mountain House Restaurant: Breakfast, lunch, and dinner with an extensive menu ranging from steaks to pasta, chicken to chicken fried steak with creamed potatoes. The country cooking includes pinto beans served with cole slaw, a wedge of onion, and corn muffins for $3.95. Closed in January. Open daily from 7:30 A.M. to 9:30 P.M. Address: 3220 Parkway. Phone: 615-453-9000.

Pop's Catfish Shack: All-you-can-eat catfish or chicken dinners with fries, slaw, hush puppies, green onions, and corn bread. Open daily 11 A.M. to 9 P.M.; weekends only, January and February. Address: 3516 Parkway. Phone: 615-428-8627.

Prime Sirloin Steak and Seafood: Choose the buffet or steaks and seafood on the menu. There's also the tempting Taco Bar . . . and homemade yeast rolls. Open Thursdays through Sundays, 11 A.M. to 10 P.M.; Fridays and Saturdays, 11 A.M. to 11 P.M. Address: 2586 Parkway. Phone: 615-428-4643.

Santos Italian Restaurant: Budget-conscious Italian food with an extensive menu ranging from chicken parmigiana for $5.95 to a muffuletta sandwich for two for $8.95. Pizza American too. Open weekdays 10 A.M. to 10 P.M.; Saturdays, 10

A.M. to 11 P.M. Closed Sundays. Address: 3271 Parkway. Phone: 615-428-5840.

Seaton's Fine Dining: A sunken dining room in the atrium of the Grand Hotel, this full-service restaurant offers a casual atmosphere with a menu that includes everything from a Smoky burger to filet mignon. A buffet also is served for breakfast, lunch, and dinner. Phone: 615-453-1000.

Trotters Restaurant: Serving breakfast, lunch, and dinner from 7 A.M. to 9 P.M., including family-style dinner featuring three meats, four vegetables, salad, and dessert. Closed December through February. Address: 3716 Parkway. Phone: 615-453-3347.

CALENDAR OF EVENTS, 1993

For more information on any specific events, contact the Pigeon Forge Department of Tourism, 1159 Parkway. P.O. Box 1390, Pigeon Forge, TN 37868. Phone: 615-453-8574; 800-251-9100 (outside Tennessee).

January

Jan. 4–10: Bridge Festival. Sectional champion-ships as well as light competition for beginners. Festival includes special instruction seminars. Held at the Holiday Inn.

Jan. 7–10: Outlet Sales. All the outlet malls offer special bargains for a three-day extravaganza.

Jan. 20–24: Wilderness Week. Wilderness ex-perts conduct walks, talks, lectures, and work-shops, free to the public. Topics range from endangered species to winter photography.

Jan. 22–23: National Fishing Lure Collectors Club at the Grand Hotel on the Parkway.

February

Feb. 20: 2nd Annual Smoky Mountain Story-telling Festival in Patriot Park, just east of the Parkway on Middlecreek Road.

Feb. 27: Pigeon Forge Shindig and Show Re-view. All the country music venues, including Dollywood, offer sneak previews of the upcom-ing season's musical reviews. At the Smoky Mountain Jubilee Theater.

March

March 6–7, June 11–21: Clogging. The Spring Fling and Smoky Mountain Classic Clogging competitions bring dancers from ages six to sixty from all over the United States. At the Grand Hotel.

April

8th Annual Southeastern Street Machine Nationals, with exotically decorated hot rods from all over the country.

April 23–26: Spring Festival and Craft Show. Handmade crafts and keepsakes on sale. Local artisans offer demonstrations of various crafts.

April 23: Dolly's Friendship Parade. Grand Marshal Dolly Parton leads an annual parade of floats and marching bands to mark the opening of Dollywood's season.

May

May 7–9: 2nd Annual "All Chevy/GMC Truck Nationals." Phone: 615-623-4644.

May 14–16: F-100s Super Nationals. Grand Hotel, 615-453-1000.

June

June 11–13: 6th Annual "Camaro/Chevelle/Nova Nationals," 615-623-4644.

June 11–13: Baseball Card Bonanza. Belz Factory Outlet Mall.

July

July 16–18: 4th Annual "Southern Mini-Truckin' Nationals," 615-623-4644.

Antique Show. Grand Hotel, 615-453-1000.

August

August 7: Midnight Road Race. No vehicles allowed in this footrace, which takes place at the stroke of midnight. A wheelchair event is included.

August 23–28: Sevier County Week. Grand Hotel, 615-453-1000.

September

Sept. 10–11: Shades of the Past. More than 2000 hot rods will be displayed in this annual event.

October

Oct. 2–31: Rotary Club Crafts Festival. Artists and crafters from across the country gather in tents in Patriot Park to demonstrate and sell their wares.

Oct. 30: Batter's Box Nascar Racing Collectibles. Grand Hotel, 615-453-1000.

November & December

Nov. 11–Feb. 28: Winterfest. Special events and spectacular Christmas lighting displays highlight this period. Now in its fourth year, the celebration is bringing more visitors, and that means more attractions—including the country music shows—are running a year-round season.

More than a half-million dollars in twinkie lights deck the town, and special events from historical tours to Christmas programs by local churches are scheduled.

DON'T MISS!! The lighting display in Patriot Park centers around a 32-foot replica of the Liberty Bell. Visitors can walk through the bell, which plays carillon chimes.

LODGING

Basic facts to keep in mind when you're making reservations in advance, essential during the peak season for visitors that runs from June through October:

Many of the motels and cabins require a minimum two-night stay with a $50 deposit on reservations. Many will not give refunds without four weeks' written notice of cancellation, so firm up plans before you call.

BUDGET ALERT!! Be sure to double-check the room rates at the time you make reservations, because most fluctuate depending on the time of year, the activities in town and holidays. (See the Pigeon Forge Calendar of Events.) Rates are lowest January through March, highest July through October. Prices can vary from $18 in January to $89 in October for the same room.

* Weekend prices are higher than weekday prices.
* Most offer senior discounts and group rates.
* Very few places take pets.

★ Some Bed & Breakfasts prefer adults only. Special advance arrangements should be made for children.

★ Accommodations are open year-round unless otherwise noted.

★ Bed & Breakfast accommodation price includes breakfasts.

★ Facilities are accessible for the handicapped unless otherwise noted. Primarily the restrictions are among some of the Bed & Breakfasts.

★ Unless noted otherwise, all accommodations accept major credit cards including Visa, MasterCard, Discover, and American Express.

★ Prices listed do not include state sales tax of $8^1/_2$ percent plus a 2 percent motel tax.

Hotels/Motels

Best Western Plaza Inn: On the Parkway at the turn-off to Dollywood, the motel offers indoor and outdoor swimming pools and hot tubs, in-room refrigerators, and free movies. Two people, $49 to $79 per night. The Executive Suite, at $195 per night for two people, offers two Jacuzzis, a king-sized bed, living and dining areas, and a fully equipped kitchen. P.O. Box 926, Pigeon

Forge, TN 37868. Phone: 615-453-5538, 1-800-232-5656.

Best Western Toni Motel: The Toni offers heated indoor and outdoor pools, and hot tubs and a sauna. King, queen, and water beds and suites are available. Two people, $48 to $110. Address: 3810 Parkway, Pigeon Forge, TN 37863. Phone: 615-453-9058; 1-800-422-3232.

Colonial House Motel: On the Parkway, the motel offers rooms with a view of the Little Pigeon River and picnic sites along the bank. Rooms with Jacuzzis, kitchens, and fireplaces also are available. Two people, $49 to $59. Address: 3545 Parkway, Pigeon Forge, TN 37863. Phone: 615-453-0717; 1-800-662-5444.

Days Inn: Midway on the Parkway, some of the 120 rooms include refrigerators. Suites are available with Jacuzzis. Outdoor heated pool. Two people, $44 to $78; suites from $48 to $98. P.O. Box 1230, Pigeon Forge, TN 37863. Phone: 615-453-4707; 1-800-325-2525.

Family Inns of America: Four Family Inns to choose from. Each offers heated outdoor pools. Some have kitchenette units available. Two people, $33 to $68. Phone: 1-800-251-9752.

Grand Hotel and Convention Center: This five-story hotel features 425 rooms and suites. Some rooms include fireplaces, Jacuzzis, saunas, kitchenettes, and water beds. A five-story waterfall trickles beside the indoor hot tub. The hotel also has indoor and outdoor heated swimming pools. In the hotel, Seaton's Fine Dining offers everything from burgers to daily buffets. Two people, $45.77 to $59.77. Address: 500 Parkway. P.O. Box 10, Pigeon Forge, TN 37868. Phone: 615-453-1000; 1-800-251-4444.

Hampton Inn: On the Parkway next to Bob Evans Restaurant, the inn offers an indoor/outdoor pool, a game room, complimentary continental breakfast, remote control TVs with VCRs, and on-premise video rental. Rooms are available with fireplaces and Jacuzzis. Two people, $58 to $95. P.O. Box 1403, Pigeon Forge, TN 37868. Phone: 615-428-5500; 1-800-388-1727.

Holiday Inn: This 208-room hotel on the Parkway offers The Holidome, featuring a heated indoor pool, sauna, health club, and game room. Food is available at Roger's Poolside Snack Bar or Louie's Place of Dining. Two people, $33 to $89. Address: 413 Parkway, Pigeon Forge, TN 37863. Phone: 615-428-2700; 1-800-465-4329.

Holiday Terrace Motel: Forty-six units on the Parkway, offers an outdoor pool with hot tub, some rooms with refrigerators, and free coffee and doughnuts every morning. Two people, $18 to $89. P.O. Box 1367, Pigeon Forge, TN 37868. Phone: 615-453-0895; 1-800-332-2346.

Howard Johnson Lodge: This 145-room complex offers an outdoor pool with a waterfall and attached wading pool, Laundromat, game room, and snack shop. Two people, $28 to $88. P.O. Box 1110, Pigeon Forge, TN 37868. Phone: 615-453-9151; 1-800-453-6008.

Kimble Overnight Rentals: Thirteen rooms above stores on the Parkway near the Old Mill. Each unit has a Jacuzzi, refrigerator, and microwave. Two people, $75 per night. Address: 3346 Parkway, Pigeon Forge, TN 37863. Phone: 615-429-0090, 1-800-447-0911.

McAfee Motor Inn: This is a 126-room motel on the Parkway. Standard rooms include a refrigerator. Two people, $49 to $59. Suites include a Jacuzzi, wet bar, and fireplace. Two people, $59 to $89. Heated pool and hot tub. Next door to Trotters restaurant. Address: 3756 Parkway, Pigeon Forge, TN 37863. Phone: 615-453-3490, 1-800-925-4443.

Mountain Trace Inn: Just off the Parkway, these 60 units feature refrigerators, remote control TVs, and outdoor heated pool and wading pool. Units with fireplaces, whirlpools, and kitchenettes are available. Two people, $38 to $78. Address: 130 Wears Valley Road, Pigeon Forge, TN 37863. Phone: 615-453-6785; 1-800-453-6785.

Norma Dan Motel: Sixty-six new units on the Parkway, across from Shoney's South and the Dixie Stampede, offer private balconies, refrigerators, and a heated swimming and wading pool. Two people, $58 to $68. Fireplaces and in-room Jacuzzis are available. P.O. Box 56, Pigeon Forge, TN 37868. Phone: 615-453-2403; 1-800-582-7866.

Quality Inn: Indoor and outdoor pools with hot tubs come with these 160 rooms which offer private balconies and remote-control cable TV. Located at the north end of the Parkway. Two people, $29.95 to $64. Address: 2385 Parkway, Pigeon Forge, TN 37863. Phone: 615-453-4106; 1-800-228-5151.

Red Carpet Inn: On the Parkway one mile from Dollywood, the motel offers an outdoor heated pool with wading pool. Two people, $32.88 to $96. Honeymoon suites with Jacuzzis range from $79.99 to $165 per night.

River Lodge South: Picnic, barbecue, or fish on the bank of the Little Pigeon River behind this motel. Or swim in the outdoor heated pool. Some rooms are available with water beds, Jacuzzis, fireplaces, and kitchenettes. Two people, $28.50 to $92.50. Address: 344 Parkway, Pigeon Forge, TN 37863. Phone: 615-453-0783; 1-800-233-7581.

Shular Inn: On the Parkway close to three outlet malls, the inn offers single rooms as well as suites. Suites are available with fireplaces and Jacuzzis. The hotel also features an indoor pool, hot tub, and sauna. Two people, $39.95 to $99.95. Suites from $69.95 to $169.95. Address: 2708 Parkway, Pigeon Forge, TN 37863. Phone: 615-453-2700; 1-800-451-2376.

Smoky Mountain Resorts: For information or reservations at any of the following motels, write: P.O. Box 187, Pigeon Forge, TN 37868. Phone: 1-800-523-3919.

Briarstone Inn: On the Parkway next to the Smoky Mountain Pancake House, 57 rooms offer queen-sized beds and refrigerators. Outdoor pool with wading pool. Rooms with Jacuzzis and fireplaces are available. Two people, $24 to $86.

Creekstone Inn: Just off the Parkway, 112 rooms offer private balconies overlooking the Little Pigeon River. Rooms have queen-sized beds and refrigerators. Outdoor pool. Rooms with fireplaces and Jacuzzis are available. Two people, $30 to $86.

Mountain Sky Motel: Close to the Briarstone Inn, this motel offers queen-sized beds and in-room refrigerators. Outdoor pool and wading pool. Two people, $24 to $82.

Mountain Valley Lodge: At the south end of the Parkway, the 60 rooms offer refrigerators and queen-sized beds. Some suites and rooms with fireplaces and Jacuzzis are available. Outdoor pool with wading pool and hot tub. Two people, $30 to $82.

Shiloh Motel: At the north end of the Parkway, the Shiloh Motel offers queen-sized beds and refrigerators. Outdoor pool and wading pool. A convenience store and service station are on the premises. Two people, $24 to $82.

Timbers Log Motel: Just off the Parkway along the Little Pigeon River, 33 units offer the feel of sleeping in a modern log cabin. Standard units include king- or queen-sized beds. Outdoor pool. Two people, $25 to $90. Two-bedroom, two-bath suites with water beds, fireplaces, and Jacuzzis range from $100 to $150. Address: 134 Davis Road, Pigeon Forge, TN 37863. Phone: 615-428-5216; 1-800-445-1803.

Vacation Lodge: Each of the 88 rooms in this three-story motel has its own balcony. Located on the Parkway, some rooms have queen-sized beds, refrigerators, and kitchenettes. Outdoor pool. Rates for two people begin at $60. P.O.

Box 37, Pigeon Forge, TN 37868. Phone: 615-453-2640; 1-800-468-1998.

Valley Forge Inn: Private balconies, indoor and outdoor pools, are available at this motel on the Parkway. Some rooms feature fireplaces, water beds, and Jacuzzis. Close to Archie Campbell's Hee Haw Village. Two people, $24.50 to $89.50. Address: 908 Parkway, Pigeon Forge, TN 37863. Phone: 615-453-7770; 800-544-8740.

Willow Brook Lodge: Fifty-two units offer Early American decor with king- or queen-sized beds, refrigerators, remote-control cable TV, and an outdoor pool. Complimentary coffee and Danish are served in the lobby every morning. Two people, $29.95 to $68. Address: 3035 Parkway, Pigeon Forge, TN 37863. Phone: 615-453-5334; 800-765-1380.

Cabins, Cottages & Condos

For information on the following places, write: P.O. Box 1138, Pigeon Forge, TN 37868. Or call 615-428-0976; 800-662-1022.

Condos on the River: Whirlpool bath, fireplaces, swimming pool, one block off Parkway. Two people, $80–$100.

Country Oaks Cottages: Two-night reservations are required. Deluxe unit with kitchen, fireplace, and Jacuzzi, two persons, $99 per night. Standard unit, two persons, $85 per night.

River Place Condos: Just east of the Parkway, near Dollywood. Jacuzzis, fireplaces, and a common outdoor heated pool highlight these two-bedroom, two-bath units. Two people, $125 per night. Address: 410 Parkway, Pigeon Forge, TN 37863. Phone: 615-428-4440; 800-448-1936.

Shadow Ridge Vacation Villas: Four two-bedroom, two-bath villas one-half mile west of the Parkway. Each has a kitchen, spiral staircase to a master bedroom with Jacuzzi and king-sized beds, fireplace, and decks overlooking the woods. Two people, $115 per night. Address: 2675 Valley Heights Drive, Pigeon Forge, TN 37863. Phone: 615-429-5808; 800-779-5808.

Smokey Ridge Chalets and Cabins: Fifty chalets on wooded ridges with a view of the Smokies. Three miles east of the Parkway. Each unit has a fireplace, Jacuzzi, and kitchen. Also available are several two- to five-bedroom houses. These start at $125 per night. Chalets: two people $90. P.O. Box 1324, Pigeon Forge, TN 37868. Phone: 615-428-5427; 800-634-5814.

Bed & Breakfasts

Day Dreams Country Inn: Two-story hemlock and cedar log house on three wooded acres, just east of the Parkway. Enjoy a stroll through the gardens or sit on a bench by Mill Creek. Each of the six rooms is furnished with a special collection of antique furniture. Two people, from $69 to $100 per night. Address: 2720 Colonial Drive, Pigeon Forge, TN 37863. Phone: 615-428-0370; 800-377-1469.

Hilton's Bluff Bed and Breakfast Inn: Ten guest rooms, including three "special occasion" rooms, feature heart-shaped whirlpool tubs and private balconies. Options include breakfast in bed and picnic baskets. No smoking. You may bring liquor. Two people, $69 to $99. One-half mile west of the Parkway on Wears Valley Road. Not equipped for people with wheelchairs. Address: 2654 Valley Heights Drive, Pigeon Forge, TN 37863. Phone: 615-428-9765.

IMPORTANT ADDRESSES
& PHONE NUMBERS

Pigeon Forge Department of Tourism
P.O. Box 1390
1159 Parkway
Pigeon Forge, TN 37868
Phone: 615-453-8574; 800-251-9100
   (Outside Tennessee)

* Ambulance Service: 615-453-3200
* Sevier Medical Center (hospital): 615-453-7111
* Great Smoky Mountains National Park: 615-436-5615
* National Weather Service, Knoxville: 615-970-2417

HISTORY

Sevier County (pronounced "severe") was formed in 1785 as the result of an agreement between chiefs of the Cherokee Nation and John Sevier, who was governor of the State of Franklin. The treaty opened the territory south of the beautiful French Broad River to settlers, and the county was named after John Sevier.

In 1788 the government of the State of Franklin collapsed, and Sevier County settlers governed themselves until 1794.

By 1795 the territory had more inhabitants than the 60,000 required to form a state government. So, on January 11, 1796, county representatives met in Knoxville to write a constitution for the State of Tennessee. The first legislature convened in March 1796, and John Sevier was elected the first governor of Tennessee.

Today, Sevier County has four incorporated cities: Sevierville, Pigeon Forge, Gatlinburg, and Pittman Center.

Sevierville was first named "Forks of Little Pigeon," after the river that runs through the area. In 1795 it became the county seat. The courthouse clock tower features an imposing Seth Thomas clock that has been in operation for eighty years. Its four faces ring out the time every half hour. Today, Sevierville has a population of 5400.

Gatlinburg was named after Radford Gatlin, a part-time Baptist preacher who moved to the area in 1854. He bought fifty acres of land from the Ogle family, who had settled the area in 1795. Gatlin opened a general store and post office, naming the town after himself. After a five-year legal battle with the Ogles, Gatlin left the area. Current population is 3500.

The smallest town is Pittman Center, named after Reverend Eli Pittman, who helped establish a school and clinic for the Board of Home Missions of the Methodist Church. Pittman Center was incorporated in 1974.

Pigeon Forge was originally named "Fanshiers," after Richard Fanshier, one of the early settlers in 1790. Later, two sources gave the town its new name: the huge flocks of passenger pigeons that stopped at the French Broad River on their migratory flights, and the early ironworks located on the river.

During the Civil War, Pigeon Forge was a Union stronghold. Early settlers farmed and tended apple orchards. Around 1900 a logging boom hit the area, but it ended when President Calvin Coolidge established the Great Smoky Mountains National Park in 1926. Pigeon Forge's history was irreversibly changed.

Today, the largest source of revenue in Sevier County is tourism. Pigeon Forge was incorporated in 1960 and has a population of 3000.

This is the compelling and heart-rending story of Cristy Lane's life and how she overcame what seemed impossible odds. It will bring a lump to your throat, a tear to your eye, and joy to your heart.

CRISTY LANE

ONE
DAY
at a
TIME

Lee Stoller with Pete Chaney

THE #1 BESTSELLER
OVER A MILLION COPIES
IN PRINT
SOON TO BE A MAJOR
MOTION PICTURE!

CRISTY LANE: ONE DAY AT A TIME
Lee Stoller with Pete Chaney
_____ 95121-3 $4.99 U.S./$5.99 Can.

Naomi Judd and her daughter Wynonna shocked the world when they announced they'd be ending their seven-year career together. Despite her spirited performances at dozens of sold-out concerts, Naomi's battle with a life-threatening disease was forcing her into retirement—leaving Wynonna to carry on the family tradition. But this was not the first time Naomi had fought the odds and won....

Here is an honest, in-depth look at the lives of Naomi and Wynonna Judd—the early years of struggle, the superstar years as the queens of country music, and their heart-rending personal tragedies. For their millions of devoted fans, THE JUDDS is a rare glimpse into the lives of two remarkable women.

The Unauthorized Biography

BOB MILLARD

With a hillbilly twang, he sang racy honky-tonk songs
next to tender gospel ballads, and his wide-brimmed hat
was his symbol. From his dirt-poor childhood with a
domineering mother, he was driven to drugs by a crippling
spinal disease and into despair by two failed marriages.
A man of down-home faith, his salvation lay in music, the
bottle, and women. Now, including never-before-
published material on the controversial emergence of
Williams' daughter, this is the rags-to-riches story of the
first "Cadillac Cowboy." It is a tale as triumphant and as
tragic as the immortal songs he crafted before his untimely
death at age twenty-nine.

Your Cheatin' Heart
A BIOGRAPHY OF HANK WILLIAMS

CHET FLIPPO

"Flippo has managed to put flesh and blood on the
sturdy bones of the Williams legend." —*People*